The Endless Jihad...

The Mujahidin, the Taliban and Bin Laden

The Endless Jihad...
The Mujahidin, the Taliban and Bin Laden

Shaul Shay

ELMHURST COLLEGE LIBRARY

The International Policy Institute for Counter-Terrorism
at the
Interdisciplinary Center Herzliya

The Endless Jihad...
The Mujahidin, the Taliban and Bin Laden

Shaul Shay

Cover design: **Pini Hamou Studios**
Production: **Dyonon**

ISBN 965-90365-4-x

Copyright © 2002
The International Policy Institute for Counter-Terrorism
The Interdisciplinary Center Herzliya

All rights reserved.
No part of this book may be reproduced in any form or
by any means without permission in writing from the Publisher.

International Policy Institute for Counter-Terrorism
P.O.Box 167
Herzliya 46150, Israel

Table of Contents

Preface	7
Islamic Fundamentalism – Background	11
Afghanistan – The Ethnic Structure	19
Historical Background – Milestones in the Formation of Afghanistan	27
The Role of Mohammed Daoud	31
The Soviet Invasion and the Karmal Government	39
The Government of Najib (Najibullah)	42
The Fall of Najibullah's Regime and the Rise of the Mujahidin	44
Afghanistan – Islamic Opposition and the Mujahidin Movements	48
The Afghan Mujahidin Movements	52
Sunni Organizations in Afghanistan	54
Shiite Organizations in Afghanistan	55
Leaders of the Mujahidin Movements in Afghanistan	59
Military Leadership of the Mujahidin	64
The Mujahidin Regime of Rabbani	67
The Taliban Movement – Roots and Ideology	70
The Taliban and the Road to Power	76
Milestones on the Taliban's Road to Power	81
The Taliban Regime – Main Characteristics	84
The Anti-Taliban Coalition – The Northern Alliance	87
Internal Power Struggles Among the Uzbekis	91
Involvement of Outside Agents in the Civil War in Afghanistan	94
Pakistan – Afghanistan (Taliban) Relations	97

Iran – Afghanistan (Taliban) Relations	100
Diplomatic Moves to Resolve the Conflict in Afghanistan 1993-2000	102
"Afghan Terror" in the International Arena as a Reflection of Cultural Conflict	105
International Terror – Theoretical Background	110
"Cultural Terror"	115
Destruction of the Statues of Buddha at Bamian – Afghanistan – 2001	117
Afghan Terror in the International Arena	123
Epilogue	147
Notes	150
Appendix	
Appendix A – Afghanistan – Provincial Divisions	165
Appendix B – 1979 As A Watershed in the History of Afghanistan	167
Appendix C – The Taliban Regime – Central Position Holders	168
Appendix D – The Islamic Ring of Conflict	171
Appendix E – Prominent Acts of Terror Attributed to the "Afghan Alumni"	173
Index of Name and Concepts	174

Preface

On September 11, 2001, the deadliest terror attack in history was launched against the USA.

Two highjacked airplanes, one after another, crashed into the twin towers of the World Trade Center in New York and caused them to collapse. A third highjacked airplane crashed into the Pentagon in Washington and a fourth, which came down in Pennsylvania, was believed to have been headed for the Presidential retreat of Camp David.

The United States accused Osama Bin Laden, who is in hiding in Afghanistan, of being responsible for the deadly attack.

Thus were the floodlights of international interest focused on Afghanistan as the refuge and hiding place of the terrorist Bin Laden.

The USA demanded categorically that Afghanistan extradite Bin laden into its custody and simultaneously initiated the formation of a coalition, the mobilization of reserves and the dispatch of a task force to take action against Bin Laden and his hosts in Afghanistan.

A decade after the Afghan Mujahidin trounced the Soviet Union's task force in Afghanistan with the help of the USA, the Taliban are facing today a conflict with the USA that is no less serious. To comprehend the reality of 2001, however, we must examine from a historical perspective the processes that took place in Afghanistan and led to the recent occurrences. Since the 1970s, there has been a bloody civil war underway in Afghanistan, the influences and implications of which reach far beyond the borders of this divided and fragmented state. The civil war began with a struggle between the Marxist regime in Kabul, which tried to change the face of Afghan society in the spirit of Marxist doctrine, and the religious and traditional factions which constituted the vast majority in conservative and patriarchal Afghan society.

Due to the failure of the pro-Soviet regime in Afghanistan to cope with the Islamic challenge, the regime's patron, the USSR, was forced to intervene to save it, and so invaded Afghanistan in December 1979. The Soviet invasion of Afghanistan turned what was an internal conflict into a global issue and a theater of conflict between the Soviet Bloc and the West on the one hand, and between radical Islam and Communism on the other.

The USSR's direct involvement in the fighting in Afghanistan began only months after the Khomeini revolution in Iran (February 1979), and the wave of radical Islamic awakening that swept the Muslim world in its wake.

The USSR viewed the occurrences in Afghanistan and neighboring Iran as a threat to its regional interests and was also concerned by the threat of radical Islam's possible infiltration of the Muslim republics on its southern border.

Accordingly, the USSR regarded it as vital to come to the aid of the pro-Soviet regime in Afghanistan to halt the spreading wave of radical Islam and to protect its own essential interests.

The Khomeini revolution in Iran brought about the fall of the pro-Western regime which had been a central stratum of the USA's sense of regional and global security, and unleashed a crisis in relations between revolutionary Iran and the USA with the seizure of the USA embassy and American diplomats in Teheran.

The loss of the strategic foothold in Iran on the one hand, and the Soviet invasion of Afghanistan on the other, gave rise in Washington to fears of Soviet domination of the Persian Gulf region, which was a main source of the West's oil supply.

The USA therefore came to the aid of the Islamic factions in Afghanistan and even encouraged its allies in the Arab and Muslim world to do likewise, to stop Soviet expansion in the region.

An "unholy alliance" took shape on the Afghan front with a variety of radical Islamic Mujahidin organizations, Iran, Pakistan, Arab countries, the USA and the People's Republic of China joining forces. Each had their own reasons and justifications for choosing to cooperate with political and ideological rivals to keep the common enemy (the USSR) in check.

Most of the Afghan Mujahidin organizations openly declared their ideological and religious hostility to the USA and the West but the inevitability of the circumstances made them willing to form an alliance even with the "devil" to withstand the real and immediate threat posed by the USSR.

The war against the Soviets in Afghanistan quickly became defined as a Jihad (holy war) and generated a new phenomenon in the history of modern Islam, with thousands of Muslim volunteers from all over the Muslim world coming to the aid of the Afghan Mujahidin and taking active part in battle. The spirit of battle, religious excitement along with extensive military and financial aid from Arab countries and the USA enabled the Afghan Mujahidin to face the Soviet forces successfully, despite the latter's obvious technological and military advantages.

The Soviet failure in the war in Afghanistan and the state's falling into the hands of the Mujahidin were viewed by radical Islamic factors throughout the world as evidence of the victory of Islamic faith over Communist ideology. The collapse of the Soviet bloc and the USSR a short time after the withdrawal of Soviet forces from Afghanistan further supported this assumption.

The claims of radical Islamic analysts, according to whom the USSR's failure in Afghanistan brought about its demise, may seem far-fetched, but there is no doubt that this failure did influence the processes that led to the collapse of the Communist regime in the USSR.

The victory of the Mujahidin in Afghanistan did not result in the end of the civil war. After the expulsion of the Soviets and the Marxist regime in Kabul, Afghan Mujahidin factions continued their internal power struggle for control of the country.

The endless battles between the radical Islamic powers in Afghanistan, as well as the inability of any of the sides to establish an effective central government, resulted in the early 1990s in the growth of a Islamic reform movement which set its sights on putting an end to the civil war and founding an "authentic" Islamic regime in accordance with its ideology.

The Taliban movement, which had grown from within Islamic education schools in Pakistan and Afghanistan, soon became the main political and military power in Afghanistan and took control of most of the country's territory.

The Taliban imposed on the country one of the most extreme and dogmatic Islamic regimes in history, but as yet not even the Taliban has succeeded in ending the civil war; opposition movements from the ethnic minorities (Tajikis, Uzbekis, and Hazaras) continue to struggle against the Taliban regime with the aid of Iran, Russia and the Muslim republics on Afghanistan's northern border (Turkmenistan, Uzbekistan, Tajikistan).

Following the victory of the Mujahidin and the Taliban, Afghanistan became a main locus of the activities of extremist Islamic terror organizations such as Osama Bin Laden's Al Qa'idah. Islamic volunteers who had participated in the war against the Soviets, and then returned to their countries of origin, became the "spearhead" of radical Islamic movements acting to topple the regimes in their countries.

Bin Laden's terror campaign against the USA – or what he calls his Jihad against the Crusader-Jewish culture – which he orchestrates from his haven in Afghanistan, is an overt manifestation of a war of cultures and perhaps a first step toward realization of the Islamic fundamentalist slogan "neither East nor West" – in other words, with the collapse of the USSR the time has come to deal with the West.

Islamic Fundamentalism – Background

Fundamentalism is a term that has Christian, Protestant origins and was adopted in the West (by scholars, politicians, journalists) to refer to religious/ideological fanaticism, as well as to define the phenomenon of Islamic fanaticism.

Muslim religious fanatics see the use of this term in the Islamic context as a form of Western intellectual imperialism, while the term they use to describe themselves is "Islamayun" – Islamics or followers of Islam, to be distinguished from "Muslimun" which means someone whose religion is Islam but whose lifestyle may be secular.[1]

In its linguistic meaning, the word "fundamentalism" refers to the adherence to the tenets of a religious faith and to the lifestyle derived from it, and contains in its doctrine all of its revelations: adoption of the religious symbols in daily life, behavior in accordance with Islam's normative codes, or organization and activism toward preserving all these and disseminating them in society.[2]

Fundamentalist organizations, associations and movements embody by their very existence the full revelation of the phenomenon: namely an ideology that promotes its aims by political means, with fundamentalist movements being in fact ideological movements whose ideology is based on the holy writings of Islam.[3]

This kind of ideology, which has its origin in "divine revelation," motivates the rejection of all other ideologies that are the product of human thought which is perceived as intrinsically imperfect.

Expressions of this kind of rejection can be seen in slogans such as "Islam is the answer" or "neither East nor West" which are common in fundamentalist propaganda. Followers of Islam claim that "fulfilling the word of Allah on earth," or in other words the establishment of Islamic society and state, is the only remedy for human society's ills.[4]

Islamic fundamentalism is not monolithic and there are significant differences in the interpretation of Islamic history (Sunni/Shiite), in interpretation of the commandments derived from the principles of the faith and in the operative approach to ideological service.[5]

The fundamentalist movement can act in various ways, including the taking of violent actions (Jihad), detachment and withdrawal from the society of infidels (Hijrah), or as a movement that sees its destiny in investing in education and indoctrination (Da'wah). Each group has its own method.

A common denominator that unifies them all is the perception of Islam's present situation as that of a culture being lost. This perception nourishes the sense of emergency and pessimism and constitutes one of the psychological-cultural motivations for their actions.

The history of the development of Islamic fundamentalism shows that a number of events and processes contributed to shaping its approaches and perceptions:

- **The encounter with the West** – considered the root of the growth of fundamentalism and the driving force behind its present invigoration. The encounter with the West has many aspects: military, technological, scientific and economic supremacy of the West, cultural foreignness, imperialist "scheming," and modernism which despite its blessings carries with it severe repercussions for traditional life. The problems awakened by the encounter, which quickly turn into conflict, mean that it is possible to define fundamentalism as one form of coping, or as the Islamic answer to culture.[6]
- **The physical conflict with the infidels** – although this derives from the overall encounter with the West, it has important influence of its own because of the great emotional value inherent in these clashes and also because of the obvious emphasis of the inferiority of the Islamic East compared to the West.[7]
- **Conflict with the government** – including experiences which often have decisive influence on the paths of the fundamentalist movements. The persecution and oppression that governments imposed on the followers of Islam, especially imprisonment and torture, usually resulted in "temporary low profiles" but in the long term promoted renewed radicalism and activism.[8] Prison experiences taught the followers of Islam that their primary enemy is not the West, imperialism and Zionism, but their own rulers at home. This conclusion clarified the need for activism and for contending with the regime via political or forceful means to bring about its defeat.

Fundamentalism, therefore, is the demonstration of radical ideology which impugns the existing order and expresses a yearning for a more just society. This is in fact a struggle for change in the socio-economic situation as part of a comprehensive struggle for the return of Islamic nations to their authentic culture. Fundamentalism combats the failing socio-economic reality and the modernism that is unable to render the material and social expectations that it generates, and seeks a response to the ills of society in the roots of Islamic society according to authentic traditional truths rather than foreign – Western, modern – truths.

Islamic fundamentalism is not a new phenomenon. The beginning of the new era in Islam is generally perceived as its renewed encounter with Western culture which apparently began with Napoleon's invasion of Egypt at the end of the 18th century. However there are those who feel that the reawakening of Islam began before that, with the Wahabi revolt on the Arabian Peninsula, and without direct Western influence.[9]

In any case, from the 19th century we are witness to a reawakening of the Muslim world in various places as a result of the encounter with Western culture.

Despite this, the first cornerstones of the fundamentalist worldview were laid in the writings of Ibn Timea (1263-1328) which were the source of inspiration for the Wahabi renewal movements in the 18th century.

Ibn Timea developed a theory that requires rising up against and delegitimizing rulers who do not implement the Shariah, contemporary Mongolian Muslim leaders, for example.[10]

Some of his ideas were adopted by 20th century fundamentalist thinkers such as Hassan Albana, the founder of the Muslim Brotherhood Movement, Al Mawdudi, a senior Muslim thinker in India, Sayyid Qutb, one of Albana's successors in Egypt and others.

Among the prominent responses to the encounter with the West is the modernist movement which sought to adapt the values of the Muslim heritage to the modern European style worldview. This movement is usually associated with the thinking and activism of persons such as Jamal Al Din Al Afghani (died in 1897) and Mohammed Abda , the chief mufti of Egypt.[11]

The modernists tried in various ways to lead Islam toward a Western lifestyle without abandoning the values of Islam. Their success was only partial and superficial, because although it was adopted, Western lifestyle and technology did not become a satisfying substitute for faith and the original values.

As mentioned, the modernist approach did not provide an adequate response to the challenges of the encounter with the West.[12] Sunni Islamic fundamentalism began to grow in several locations simultaneously: in the Middle East (mainly Egypt) and the Indian sub-continent and, despite the geographic distance between them, there were clear similarities in their worldviews, diagnoses of the ills of Muslim society and remedies.

A main cornerstone in the development of Islamic fundamentalism was laid with the establishment of the "Muslim Brotherhood" movement (in 1929) by Hassan Albana. In the 1930s and 1940s the movement succeeded in establishing its status in Egypt and even spread throughout the Arab world. Albana called for a return to Islamic orthodoxy while demanding, in the name of Islamic values, that authorities attend to social, educational, economic and welfare problems. Albana called for full Egyptian independence (freedom from colonial rule) under a caliph who would rule in the spirit of Islamic law.[13] The way to attain this goal (over which his successors argued) was, first, by cooperating with all organizations opposing the existing regime and only afterward through seizure of power by the Muslim Brotherhood. Following Albana's death in 1949, the movement experienced a leadership crisis and internal division. His successors were unanimous regarding the goal and vision of founding an Islamic law state but divided as to the way to achieve it.

Albana's official successor, Hassan Al Hadibi (who was appointed "chief leader" of the Muslim Brotherhood in 1951) formulated a "moderate" thesis during the years he spent in Nasser's prisons. He recorded this approach in his book *Preaching and Not Judging*. The book was a response to Al Hadibi's rival Sayyid Qutb who in the same period formulated an opposing radical theory which will be described below. The school that formed around Al Hadibi's views was called "Traditional Fundamentalism" by the scholar Fuad Ajami.

This approach advocates compromise with the political reality, be it democratic or dictatorial. Realization of Islam by a believer is a personal affair and only limited areas are the territory of the Islamic rule. Al Hadibi believed that the Muslim masses should be recruited via cordial means rather than violent coercion. Information and education are therefore the central tools for repairing society.[14]

Sayyid Qutb, the radical ideologue of the Muslim Brotherhood, was influenced by the worldview of Abu A'la Mawdudi (an arbiter of religious law of Indian-Afghan origin) and his student Abu Al Hassan Al Nadawi. Mawdudi's doctrine was formulated against the background of India's protracted struggle for independence, and Mawdudi saw nationalism and the nation state as a danger to the interests and identity of the believing Muslim public. In an article that he published in 1930,[15] he claims that nationalism is not a new phenomenon and that its roots are in the ancient world (Babylon, Egypt, Persia). Nationalism has a permanent nature and historical continuity that are expressed in the 20th century in the figure of the nation state. Nationalism, according to Mawdudi, because it is based on common race, language or interests leads to conflict and return to the lack of solidarity of early Islam – the chaotic times of the Djahilia.

The nation state is therefore a negative and destructive phenomenon that divides humanity into ethnic groups and erects barriers between them. Islam on the other hand sees the world as one social system common to all human cultures and as the representation of the divine on earth.

To prove his claim, Al Mawdudi cites the success of the prophet Mohammed in mediating the tribal, family and economic conflicts that characterized the Arabian Peninsula before the rise of Islam. Al Mawdudi therefore translates the Djahilia reality of the pre-Islamic period into the concepts and the reality of modern nationalism in the 20th century.[16]

Hassan Al Nadawi develops Al Mawdudi's theory in elitist directions. In his opinion Muslims were appointed the ambassadors of God to lead the world and humanity. Islam is the supreme religion and therefore Muslims cannot be subordinated or led by members of other religions. Al Nadawi therefore rejects cooperation with members of other religions in the attempt to change society, denies non-Islamic perspectives and is convinced that Islam's return to dominance over human culture is an inevitable determinist process.[17]

Sayyid Qutb's position was formulated under the influence of the Muslim Brotherhood's failure to cope with the Nasser regime in Egypt. The failure brought Qutb to the ideas of **Tahfir, Hijrah, Talia** and **modern Djahilia**, which together led Islamic fundamentalism to an uncompromising struggle with government.

The roots of some of these ideas are in the writings of Ibn Timea while others are based on the writings of Abul A'la Almawdudi.[18] Sayyid Qutb describes reality in terms of neo-Djahilia, while classical Islam perceives the Djahilia (period of ignorance) as restricted to permanent defined periods of time – the period before the appearance of Islam on the Arabian Peninsula.[19]

Sayyid Qutb inserts new and current content into the concept of the Djahilia and extends its significance to all of human history.[20] "Today's world lives in Djahilia from which derive all life's principles and orders...the Djahilia is not a period in time, but a situation of the kind that we have borne whenever society digressed from the path of Islam, in the past, present and future as well".[21]

Qutb defines the Djahilia as follows: "The Djahilian society is any society that is not Islamic and, put objectively, any society that does not direct its servitude to God alone..servitude embodied by faith, ritual and legislation."[22]

This definition includes all the Djahilia societies that exist today. In Sayyid Qutb's opinion most of their intellectual and material "yields" were Djahilian anyway, even when they appeared praiseworthy and respectable.[23]

Neo-Djahilia, despite being universal, is largely focused on Western civilization which Qutb refers to as an integrative whole that includes Christianity, Communism and Judaism, with Islamic civilization having secondary status.

Although these cultures are but a single component in the composite human culture, Qutb sees them as a mirror of the whole world and chooses to focus on them.[24]

Qutb claims that Muslim society is divided into two categories: societies that declare their secularism (Almaniah) and lack of religious piety, and societies that declare their "respect for religion" but in practice remove it from the context of their social lives. Qutb feels that any Muslim society that does not base itself upon the laws and lifestyles of divine judgement ("Al Hachmiya Al Alohiya") and Shariah deserves its place as part of the modern Djahilia.[25]

Sayyid Qutb and his brothers draw an analogy between the power of neo-Djahilia and classical Djahilia. In their view, there is no question about the "supremacy and seniority" of the former, not only in its geographic distribution and but also in the extent and seriousness of its crimes.

"20th century Djahilia – in reality – is the cruelest Djahalia in human history on the face of the earth,"[26] therefore the efforts required by the Prophet in the past to confront his enemies were minimal compared to those required in the present and in the future to eliminate evil. In the present and future, believers will be required to fight a double enemy: the external one (mainly Western culture) and the internal one within the Muslim world.[27]

According to the principle of **Tahfir,** the society in which the Muslim lives is tainted with corruption and infidelity and therefore it is forbidden to cooperate and join forces with its components. The Muslim believer must fight this society and its rulers to return society to Islamic values. The struggle against society and its leaders will take place by means of **Talian** rescue forces which will use all means, including violence, to establish a traditional Islamic state.

According to Qutb the principle of **Hijrah** can also be used as the prophet Mohammed used it in 622 BCE when he was forced to leave Djahilian Mecca and settle in Medina. This move can be replicated in a modern version, not by means of emigrating from a country but by "conceptual and behavioral "emigration." Qutb sees separatism only as the first stage of emotional and spiritual preparation and believes that direct action and violent struggle must be undertaken later.[28]

The writings of Sayyid Qutb exhibit not only the desire to attest to the hardships and needs of the real Islam in its struggle against neo-Djahilia but also attempt to perform philosophical and historical research into the foundations of Western culture.[29]

Studies of the West by such thinkers as Sayyid Qutb do not presume to be objective or "fair," but to reveal the weaknesses and ills inherent in Western culture and, by denying its validity, lead the reader to the conclusion that there is no alternative but Islam.[30]

Sayyid Qutb characterizes the malaise of Muslim society, analyses it and its components and reaches the conclusion that only activism, Jihad and revolution by "true believers" are likely to effect a reversal of the dark reality he experienced and bring about the establishment of a traditional Islamic state.[31]

Mustafa Shakri, the founder Misad El Hijrah, El Takfir, and Abd Alsalem Frej (among the founders of the Islamic Jihad in Egypt), Qutb's ideological successors, developed his radical line and adopted the ideology and modes of Jihad action against the regime and its supporters to bring about in the shortest time (in their opinion) the demise of "corrupt regimes" and establish a traditional Islamic state. Qutb's inheritors reject modern Islamic apologetics and "imported" ideological ideas such as democracy, socialism or nationalism, while in their eyes there is only authentic, pure, Islam, free of foreign influences. Therefore, they are obligated to build an alternative society on the ruins of the Djahilian society by means of information and education of the masses, on the one hand, and a violent and uncompromising struggle against whoever stands in their way, on the other.[32]

At the end of the 1950s, the Shiite awakening began. Shiite fundamentalism as an ideological-political movement began to develop in the religious centers of Najaf and spread its influence to the Shiite populations in Iran and Lebanon. In the 1960s and 1970s, Najaf became the intellectual-revolutionary "melting pot" where the radical worldview of the religious clerics from Lebanon who eventually became the leaders of Hizbullah was forged.

The Shiite fundamentalist awakening is part of the general phenomenon of Islamic fundamentalism, the roots of which we have already considered. But Shiism is unique in its sense of historical affront which is a result not only of lagging behind and being discriminated against in the West but also of Shiites being an oppressed minority within the Muslim world for hundreds of years.[33]

The sense of inferiority is built into the "foundational mythos" of Shiism which is based on the injustice perpetrated on the house of Ali after the death of the prophet, in that he was robbed of his right to rule Islam. The dispute with the Sunni and the sense of continuing political, social and economic discrimination, lent force and power to Shiite fundamentalism since it awakened and burst onto the scene with the actions of Khomeini.

Khomeini's main contribution to Islamic political thought was the idea of the rule of the Muslim religious sage.[34]

Khomeini claimed that if a ruler was loyal to Islam, he had to be subordinate to pakiya and consult with them on the laws of Islam to be able to fulfill them. Therefore the real leaders are the spiritual leaders and the government must obey them.[35]

The new significance that Khomeini gave to Shiism includes faith in immediate messianic redemption which can be promoted through political activity. Therefore redemption must be worked for rather than waited for. According to the new Shiism, religious doctrines and symbols are perceived as means to a political struggle while, not only is there no distinction between religion and politics, even the most ceremonial aspects of Shiite Islam (such as Ashura) have political significance. For Khomeini, Ashura (which is meant to commemorate the tragedy of the battle of Karbala) became a symbol of political activism and self-sacrifice in the battle of Shiism against its enemies.

To adopt this activism, modern Shiites had to move far from the founding principle that characterized Shiism until the last century – the principle of Tiaqya (external non-Shiite appearance). Instead of the Tiaqya, Khomeini's doctrine posits Jihad to repair the historical injustice perpetrated on the Shiites and reinstate the glory of Islam.[36]

Afghanistan – The Ethnic Structure

Afghanistan is located at a strategic crossroads in the center of Asia between the former Soviet Union to the north (today Tajikistan, Uzbekistan and Turkmenistan), China to the east, Pakistan to the east and south and Iran to the west.

Throughout history, Afghanistan geopolitical position has made it a theater of war and conquests by regional rulers and imperialist powers.

Its present borders were determined by agreements signed by foreign powers and not according to the ethnic or nationalist identity of the population in these regions. The official borders of Afghanistan therefore transverse the traditional areas of settlement of various ethnic groups and four main ethnic groups are included in its territory:[1]

1. The Pashtuns – in the center and south of the country, are the largest ethnic group in Afghanistan. The remainder of the Pashtun live in Pakistan.
2. The Tajikis – in the northeast of the country, with most of the Tajiki population resident in neighboring Tajikistan.
3. The Uzbekis – in the northwest of the country, with most of the Uzbeki population resident in neighboring Uzbekistan.
4. The Hazaras – in the central north and northwest of the country, with the rest of the population resident in Iran.

In addition to the large ethnic groups there are tens of other ethnic groups that contribute to the heterogeneity of Afghan society.

The majority of the Afghan population is Sunni Muslim (approximately 85%) with Shiite Muslims making up approximately 14% and members of other religions another 1% of the total population.[2]

Since 1936 the official languages of Afghanistan have been Pashtun (Pushtun) and Farsi and the alphabet is Arabic. But in addition to the official languages different populations in Afghanistan speak 49 different languages or dialects according to their ethnic and tribal affiliation.[3]

Most of the Afghani population is rural and lives from agriculture, sheep raising, carpet weaving and trade. In the second half of the 1960s there was a significant increase in the urban population mainly around the capital city Kabul and in a number of other central provincial cities.

The Afghan civil war brought about a rise in urban populations in the wake of rural inhabitants fleeing embattled areas and the destruction of agricultural infrastructure.

As a result of the civil war millions of Afghan residents fled across the country's borders and settled in refugee camps in Pakistan and Iran. The number of Afghan refugees is estimated at 5 million.[4]

Most of Afghanistan is characterized by mountainous and desert areas that make contact and transportation between different areas difficult. Therefore, Afghan society developed into an ethnically, tribally and regionally divided society and the central government in Kabul had wavering control over the periphery.

For most of its history Afghan society kept its traditional patriarchal culture with patron/client patterns and strong bonds to the basic status group known as Qawm.[5]

This term refers to a sector of society which could be a clan, extended family, village, etc. The clan defined as Qawm is built on a sense of affiliation, patron/client relations and group solidarity which defends its members against outside threats.

Islam is the main common denominator between most sectors of Afghan society but the common faith is not enough to consolidate a collective identity that would bridge the conflicts of interest and rivalries between various groups.[6]

The Pashtuns are the largest ethnic group among the Afghan population and throughout most of history they held most of the rule and positions of power in the country, in rivalry with other ethnic minorities.

The Pashtuns

Pashtuns, as noted, comprise the largest ethnic group in Afghanistan. The vast majority of Pashtuns are Sunni Muslim and speak Pashtun.

Since the establishment of Afghanistan by Ahmed Shah in 1747 the country has traditionally been ruled by the Pashtuns. According to the latest population census, held in 1978, the Pashtuns comprised 40% of the total population.[7]

During the Communist regime and the Soviet conquest, a rift occurred in the Pashtun population between the ruling party (and all its factions) with most of its supporters coming from the Pashtun population and most of the Mujahidin movements that fought against the Communist regime whose supporters also derived from this population.

The Pashtuns paid the heaviest price in the civil war, both in the rate of casualties amongst its ranks on both sides and in the fleeing of close to 5 million refugees to Pakistan and Iran, most of whom were Pashtun.

The mass emigration of the Pashtun population resulted in a temporary change in the demographic balance in 1979-1990, when the Pashtun sector of the population declined to 30%.[8]

The process changed starting in 1990 when some refugees began returning to Afghanistan. Pashtun society is characterized by social division and segmentation, mainly on the basis of tribal and local affiliations.

Pashtun society was therefore torn not only between Communism and the Islamic Mujahidin, but also between two main streams, creating serious political and military power struggles.

The Communist movement, which was largely based on the Pashtuns, was divided into two camps, the Khalq and the Parcham, which fought against each other during most of the years of Communist rule. Within the Islamic camp, the Pashtun population split into tens of political and military groups mainly on the basis of personal and tribal loyalties.

During the struggle against the Communist regime most of the organizations and movements eventually melded into eight main Mujahidin movements which engaged in endless power struggles amongst themselves.

As the dominant, ruling ethnic group for most of Afghan history, the Pashtuns were in perpetual conflict with most of the ethnic minorities, especially the Tajikis and Uzbekis in the north and the Shiites in the center and west.

These minorities occasionally took advantage of the splits and divisions amongst the Pashtuns to further their own status and power in the Afghan political and economic system.

The Pashtuns in Afghanistan maintain close ties with the large Pashtun minority in neighboring Pakistan. The Durand Agreement between Afghanistan and Britain led to the demarcation of the official border between Pakistan and Afghanistan which is valid today, and which divided the Pashtun population between the two countries. Afghanistan does not recognize this border, but because of the ongoing civil war and the need for Pakistan's assistance this issue has been shelved. The idea however, of "Pashtunistan" comes up from time to time in various Pashtun circles.[9]

The Tajikis

The Tajiki population, comprising 25% of Afghanistan's population. Most Tajikis are Sunni Muslims, with the exception of a small minority group of Shiite Ismaelis, who mostly reside near the city of Herat. The Tajiki population is concentrated mainly in the mountainous regions in the northeast of the country, as well as in western Afghanistan and the capital Kabul.

Tajikis speak Farsi but use the Arabic alphabet. The Tajikis represent the more affluent, better-educated sector of the Afghanistan population and, therefore, traditionally held influential and powerful positions in administration, public service, commerce and economics. In rural areas, the Tajikis mainly dealt in agriculture and shepherding. The Tajikis have no defined hierarchical social structure and therefore tended to adopt the structure and social behavior of their neighbors.

Tajikis traditionally constitute the second largest ethnic minority after the Pashtuns and, therefore, there is an entrenched rivalry between them for positions of power and control of the country. Nevertheless, with the exception of two short periods, one in the 14th century and the second for about 10 months in 1929, the Tajikis have never ruled the areas of the country that they inhabit.[10] Rivalry between the Tajikis and the Pashtuns worsened in the 19th century because of attempts by the central regime in Kabul to implement "Pashtunization",[11] encouragement of Pashtun settlement in areas dominated by Tajikis and Uzbekis. (The Pashtun settlers were called Nakil – "the excommunicated" in local parlance.)

The central regime in Kabul did not succeed in changing the demographic balance in the northern provinces but did deepen the hostility and rivalry between the ethnic minorities in the largely Pashtun north.

During the period of Communist rule of Afghanistan from 1965-1979 and later during the period of the Soviet conquest, the Tajiki population was expelled from its influential positions in Kabul by various factions of the Communist party, which were totally controlled by Pashtuns. Further, the influence of the central regime and Soviet conquering forces in Tajiki dominated areas was less than in other regions, because of the mountainous terrain that hindered Soviet military activity and enabled the Mujahidin to retain autonomous rule of most of the region.

Most of the Tajiki population therefore identified with the resistance movements against the Communist regime. However, unlike the Pashtun population of which a significant percent was forced to flee to neighboring Pakistan, only 6% of the Afghan refugees were members of the Tajiki minority.

As a result of the mass emigration of Afghan refugees (most of them Pashtun) to neighboring countries, a change occurred in the demographic balance in Afghanistan; between 1979 and 1990, Tajikis constituted 33% of the population.[12] This demographic change had great significance during various stages of Communist rule and the victory of the Mujahidin.

From 1990, with the return of some of the Afghan refugees, the demographic balance again shifted and the Tajikis became only 25% of the population.

The Uzbekis

Most Uzbekis are Sunni Muslims and speak the Uzbeki language, which belongs to the Turkish linguistic family.

Uzbekis came to Afghanistan mainly in two periods. The first influx was in the 16th century with the invasion by Uzbeki tribes of the northern territories (north and south of the Amu Darya river) in what is today Afghanistan. The second wave, in the 20th century, followed the rise of the Soviet regime, the establishment of the USSR and persecution of ethnic minorities.

The Uzbeki population is concentrated in the north and west of the country, mainly in the provinces of Quaisan and Maimana. They usually coexist peacefully with the Tajiki population and intermarriages between the two minorities are quite common.

Uzbekis are divided into two classes: the more established population which is called "Asli" (the originals) and the newer population which is called "Mahajrun" (the immigrants).

During the Communist rule and the Soviet conquest of Afghanistan, most Uzbekis took a neutral stand in the conflict between the regime and the resistance movement. Therefore, Uzbeki areas were less damaged by the civil war than other regions.

Uzbeki intelligentsia were more influenced by secular and nationalist ideologies (such as Panturkism) and less by radical Islamic notions and adherence to Islam. The Muslim way of life was associated mainly with lower socioeconomic classes.

It is significant that throughout the civil war no Uzbeki Mujahidin movements developed; Uzbekis who wanted to join the struggle mostly joined the Tajiki Mujahidin (the Islamic Jamiat) movement.[13]

Moreover, the principal military component of the population served in the

Afghan army in a division commanded by the Uzbeki General Dostum and largely based on recruitment from this population sector.

When the Mujahidin besieged Kabul in 1992, General Dostum defected to the Mujahidin and helped to destroy the Najibullah regime.

Following his association with the Mujahidin coalition, General Dostum gained control of the northern Uzbeki inhabited provinces and established almost full autonomy under his leadership.

Between 1992 and 1994, Dostum's militia was a significant force in the battles between the Rabani government and his rivals, Hekmatyar, the Pashtun and the Shiite organizations.

The Hazaras (Shiite minority)

The Hazara population of Afghanistan numbers some 1.480 million inhabitants (as of 1995). The Hazaras are Farsi-speaking Shiites that live in the center and west of Afghanistan, mainly in the region known as Hazarajat.[14] They most likely came to Afghanistan in the 13th century with the conquests of Genghis Khan of Mongolia.

Hazaras settled in the harshest subsistence areas and live a traditional life of herding and agriculture. In adapting to the cold climate in these mountainous regions, a large number of Hazaras migrate from the hills to the valleys and back again with the changing seasons. Because of the difficult living conditions in the regions they inhabit, many Hazaras have moved to urban areas and earn their living from irregular jobs. The Hazaras are among the poorest and weakest populations in Afghanistan. They were discriminated against by central rulers through most of history because of their ethnic identity and Shiite faith. During Communist rule the Hazaras were among the first to rise up against the central government and managed to preserve almost full autonomy in the regions they dominated for most of the civil war years.

Because of its geographic and social isolation, the Hazara society preserved traditional patterns of rule and social stratification with communities being ruled by a Khan or Malek, because of their social and political standing, and a Sayyid as the religious leader of the community.[15]

Hazara society has remained homogenous and intermarriages between them and other ethnic groups are rare.

During the civil war many Hazaras were forced to flee to Iran where they continued to assist and enlist in the ranks of the Shiite Mujahidin movements.

The Hazara Mujahidin received military and economic aid from the Iranians during the struggle against the Communist regime and afterwards during the power struggles with other Mujahidin.

In conclusion, social, ethnic and tribal realities, the lack of political stability and the absence of an effective central government led to the development of autonomous communities that to a large degree preserved their uniqueness, the nature of their cultures and their languages.

The attempt at a Marxist regime in Kabul marked, at the end of the 1960s, the beginning of fundamental changes in all aspects of life in Afghan society including undermining Islam's standing as the foundation of personal and social life. It engendered stubborn resistance on the part of traditional populations and a serious rift in Afghan society, which had hitherto been no less complex and segmented.

Historical Background – Milestones in the Formation of Afghanistan

The history of Afghanistan has been decisively influenced by its geopolitical position and status, especially its location as the site of a struggle between the Russian empire (and later the USSR) and Britain (and the West). Afghanistan's formation began in 1747 when Nadir Shah, the ruler of Iran – of which Afghanistan at that time was a province – was assassinated. One of his military commanders by the name of Ahmed Khan took advantage of the opportunity, gathered the Pashtun tribes (the largest ethnic group in the region) around him and established an independent principality with its capital in Kandahar, where he ruled until 1773. Ahmed Khan laid the foundation for the dynasty of Afghanistan's rulers. He took the title Ahmed Khan Dur-Durani or in short Durani,[1] a name which was associated with the tribal coalition that he headed and became the name of the dynasty that ruled Afghanistan until 1973.

During the years of his rule Ahmed Khan succeeded in unifying the tribes and laying the preliminary foundations for establishment of the Pashtun state, but the principality broke down during the period of his successors from the Saduzai family. The kingdom was reunited only after an uprising brought another descendent of the Durani dynasty, Dost Mohammed Khan, to power.

Dost Mohammed was the first to call himself the Emir of Afghanistan, and during his rule from 1835-1863 important steps were taken towards unification of the country. But more than anything, his period was distinguished by his attempt to preserve the independent Afghan entity in the context of power struggles between the British and Russian empires, struggles which were known as "the great game".[2]

Consolidation of the Pashtun ethnic minority and growing Russian involvement in Afghanistan gave rise to British concern over the possible impact of developments in Afghanistan on the stability of British rule, particularly in areas of India populated by the Pashtun (which are today part of Pakistan). In 1838 the British invaded Afghanistan and the first Anglo-Afghan war began (one of three wars that took place between 1838-1919).

The Anglo-Afghan wars were a formative experience for the Afghani national ethos because, despite the political and military superiority of the British Empire and its victory, a common tribal uprising occurred in the battlefields in Afghanistan that brought the British to the conclusion that the price of their remaining in Afghanistan would be too high. They therefore withdrew their forces from Afghanistan in 1842. A similar process occurred in 1880 (the second Anglo-Afghan war 1879-1880).

In 1880 Abed el Rahman Khan was crowned king of Afghanistan and ruled the country until 1901. During these years the borders of Afghanistan were outlined under British and Russian duress. The Durand Agreement was signed on November 12, 1893, according to which the northern side of the Amu Darya river became the border between Afghanistan and Russia, while extensive parts of eastern and southern Afghanistan were transferred to British rule (the Durand line). As a result, half of the Pashtun population were cut off from Afghanistan.

Abed El Rahman Khan made serious attempts during his rule to consolidate central government and unify the country. Part of this effort involved working to weaken tribal influence and formulate a central concentrated Afghan administration. He also worked to disseminate Islam in the mountainous regions of the Hindu-Kush ranges among largely pagan populations.

Another significant milestone in Afghan history occurred in 1919 with the rise to the throne of Amanullah Khan, who felt the time was ripe to achieve full independence for his country. On April 13, 1919, he declared the independence of Afghanistan.

Thus began the third Anglo-Afghani war – a time in which Afghanis suffered many failures on the battlefield but Britain, mainly for political reasons, was forced to officially recognize the independence of Afghanistan (the Rawalpindi Agreement, August 8,1919).

The rule of Amanullah Khan was notable for its Western-style social and economic reform programs, which echoed processes occurring in other Muslim countries in the Middle East – for example, Attaturk's reforms in Turkey, and reform in Iran and Egypt. In 1923 Amanullah Khan convened a Loya Girga (convocation of tribal and religious leaders), which formulated and adopted

Afghanistan's first constitution. Later Amanullah Khan abolished slavery, granted rights to women and cancelled the obligation of Hijab.

These reforms, however, met with sharp resistance from the traditional elite and the rural Afghani population which was not ready for the processes of Westernization. An uprising erupted in the rural villages that quickly spread to most of the country's territories.

The conflict between Amanullah Khan's regime, which tried to implement reform and change Afghan society, and the traditional powers, especially religious ones, is one of the cornerstones for understanding the events of fifty years later, since this was the first time that opponents of the government declared their struggle a **Jihad** – in other words, a holy war against an oppressive ruler who deviated from the commandments of Islam.[3]

The USSR was the first power to recognize the independence of Afghanistan and institute diplomatic relations. It even provided the country with economic and military aid. On November 28, 1921, the first Soviet-Afghani cooperation agreement was signed and on August 31, 1926, another agreement of neutrality and non-aggression was signed.

The friendly relations between the USSR and Amanullah Khan's regime resulted in the first Soviet attempt at military intervention in Afghanistan in 1929, when Stalin sent a Soviet military force in an attempt to save Amanullah Khan's regime.

The Soviets sent 1000 troops from the Red Army, dressed in Afghan army uniforms, under the command of the military attaché in Afghanistan, Primakov.

The unit crossed the Amu Darya river and reached the Mazar-e-Sharif region from where it planned to advance toward Kabul. However, it stopped on Stalin's orders after he heard that Amanullah Khan had fled Kabul for India.

The Soviet forces withdrew to the USSR in an action which cost the lives of 8,000 Afghan soldiers and 120 Soviets.

On January 14, 1929, Amanullah Khan was forced to resign, forfeit his throne and flee his country following a military coup. A period of political instability lasting until 1933 descended on Afghanistan.

After Amanullah Khan, Afghanistan was ruled for a short time (some nine months) by the leader of the Islamic rebels Batche Sakao, a member of the Tajiki minority who declared himself Emir. He was deposed by General Nadir Khan and later executed (October 1929).

Nadir Khan, who crowned himself king of Afghanistan, did not last long as a ruler and was assassinated in 1933 in his palace in Kabul.

On November 8, 1933, Zahir Khan of the Durani dynasty came to power in Afghanistan and was crowned king (King Zahir Shah).

In 1946, Zahir Shah founded a constitutional kingdom in Afghanistan and in 1949 the first parliamentary elections were held.

The failure of Amanullah Khan's reforms provided an important lesson learned and implemented by the rulers of Afghanistan in the years that followed, and the central government made every effort to avoid friction with the traditional establishment and peripheral tribal system. Consequently, the influence and control of the central government over the periphery was minimized, and the hegemony of the tribal system and local leadership was preserved through extensive autonomy in these regions.[4] The separation between the central government and the periphery prevented development of an infrastructure of services and a modern economic system and most of Afghani society was fixed in place as a patriarchal tribal system based on traditional sources of income (agriculture, sheep raising, carpet weaving, etc.).

There is no doubt that this tradition of rule had a decisive impact on the social and political realities when in 1978 the socialist-oriented regime attempted to implement far-reaching reforms for changing the face of Afghan society.

The Rule of Mohammed Daoud

Mohammed Daoud, cousin of King Mohammed Zahir Shah, who served as prime minister from 1953-1963 was a key figure in the Afghan political system.

Daoud advocated drawing closer to the USSR, expanding cooperation with it and formulating reforms in the spirit of socialism that would reshape Afghan society. During his term as prime minister, he expanded military, economic and political cooperation with the USSR. Important infrastructure projects were carried out with Soviet aid, including the paving of a road system to connect the cities of Afghanistan, the Afghan army was supplied with modern Soviet manufactured weaponry and thousands of officers were trained in the USSR.

In 1963 Mohammed Daoud resigned as prime minister due to differences of opinion with King Zahir and abandoned the political arena. He continued to work behind the scenes, however, and waited for an opportunity to seize power.

His chance arose on July 17, 1973, when King Zahir was visiting Europe. With the aid of factions in the military and the support of "left-wing organizations" in Afghanistan he deposed the king, declared Afghanistan a republic and appointed himself its president.

Daoud began his rule with a series of economic and social reforms, including agrarian reform, with the blessing of the USSR. These, however, were met with resistance from the traditional elite in the rural provinces and indifference from the farmers who were supposed to benefit from them.

From 1973-1975 Daoud's "enthusiasm" for implementing reforms faded and he gradually began to adopt more pragmatic policies in an attempt to appease the traditional elite and the old establishment.

At the same time, Daoud revised his foreign policy, deciding to minimize his dependence on the USSR and work towards improving relations with the USA, Pakistan and Saudi Arabia.

In April 1975 he visited Iran, after which Afghanistan received loans and economic aid from that country.[1] The following was said of Daoud because of his "balanced" policy toward the two superpowers: "Daoud was happiest when he could light his American cigarette with a Soviet match."

Daoud's attempts to win the favor of the Afghan people resulted in the demand for national recognition for the Pashtun and Balutchi in Pakistan. This policy created tensions in the relations between Afghanistan and Pakistan, and an attempt on the part of the latter to organize a conspiracy to bring down Daoud's regime. The attempt failed; most of the conspirators were caught and executed. Daoud undertook to purge the senior leadership and appointed a new cabinet.

On August 20, 1975, Daoud embarked on a reconciliation visit to Pakistan. In talks with the Pakistani president, Ali Bahutu, he reached understandings on controversial issues and removed, at least temporarily, the Pakistani threat to his regime. In that same year Daoud continued drawing closer to the West and sent his brother, Prince Mohammed Naim, to Washington to try to improve relations with the USA.

In the early 1960s, a number of socialist-oriented movements began organizing in the Afghan political system which, during the 1970s, played a central role in shaping Afghan society.

The most prominent among these movements was the National Party (Khalq) which was founded in 1965 by Nour Mohammed Taraki. His party had a socialist bent and advocated taking radical steps toward change in Afghan society that included agrarian reform, nationalization of property and factories and their transfer to public ownership, and Afghanistan's joining the socialist movement.

In the 1960s and early 1970s these movements were the main source of support for Daoud's socialist policies.

The 1976 elections left their mark on Afghanistan's political system. The National Party (Khalq) suffered a resounding failure, causing it to change gears. It abandoned public activity and moved to clandestine organization, establishing cadres in the military, the middle ranks of public service, the urban intelligentsia and the working class.[2]

In the same year a split occurred in the Khalq and a group led by Babrak Karmal broke away from the party to establish a new movement called Parcham, which means "banner." Karmal advocated a more pragmatic approach and continued political activity according to the parliamentary "rules of the game," a policy that caused opponents of his movement among the Khalq to call it "the Royal Communist Party."

Because of his pro-Western turnabout, Daoud's relations with the Parcham movement, which was his main ally but had begun to criticize his government's policies, became shaky.

Rising pressure at home from the left-wing parties and a desire to maintain solid relations with his neighbor and patron the USSR, caused Daoud to pay a visit to Moscow in 1977.

During the visit, President Brezhnev of the USSR demanded that Daoud change his pro-Western policy. By refusing to comply, Daoud appears to have sealed his fate. The USSR began to plot the moves that would bring about his downfall a year later.[3]

In July 1977 (apparently on USSR orders), Babrak Karmal, leader of the Parcham, officially and publicly joined the ranks of the opposition to Daoud's government and the Parcham movement united with the radical Khalq. Together they established the People's Democratic Party of Afghanistan[4] with Nour Mohammed Taraki appointed as General Secretary.

In April 1978 a senior Parcham activist was murdered in Kabul. The movement's leaders accused the minister of the interior Abdel Kader Nuristani and Daoud of being responsible for the murder, and the funeral was accompanied by mass anti-establishment and anti-American demonstrations. Another version pointed to Hafizullah Amin as initiator of the murder as part of his struggle for party leadership. In any case, the public outcry and demonstrations lent legitimacy to the coup d'état that subsequently occurred.

Daoud concluded that he had to act quickly to suppress the power of the leftist parties. Shortly thereafter, a wave of arrests of left-wing activists ensued, but before Daoud managed to arrest the leaders of the parties, the Khalq mobilized under the leadership of Hafizullah Amin. With support from within the military, he effected a coup on April 27, 1978, and seized the government. Daoud, together with thirty members of his family and followers, was executed.

On April 30, 1978, the military coup council issued Declaration No.1 which stated that the council would transfer its authority to a revolutionary council which would be declared the supreme ruling body of Afghanistan, with the military council comprising part of it. Afghanistan was declared the Democratic Republic of Afghanistan.

The Khalq and the Parcham established a new government and appointed Nour Mohammed Taraki, leader of the Khalq, as president of the revolutionary council and Prime Minister of the Democratic Republic of Afghanistan. Babrak Karmal of the Parcham and Hafizullah Amin of the Khalq were appointed deputy prime ministers to maintain equilibrium between the Khalq and the Parcham in the new cabinet.

The revolutionary council's first tasks were to establish a new governmental and legal system, appoint provincial governors and senior commanders for the army, and change the three-colored national flag to a red flag similar to that of the Soviet's but bearing the symbol of Afghanistan. The coup of April 1978 was apparently neither ideologically motivated nor the result of extreme socio-economic circumstances, but mainly motivated by political power considerations.[5]

The alliance between the Khalq and Parcham primarily reflected short-term common needs and interests, but could not bridge the ideological gaps and personal rivalries for long. Although most of its leaders had had Western contacts in the past[6] the Khalq was the more radical of the two movements and advocated Maoist approaches. The Khalq aspired, by revolutionary means, to change Afghan society from a feudal theocracy to a socialist society. This contrasted with the Parcham movement, which was closer to Soviet Communist orthodoxy both ideologically and politically. Although the Parcham leaders also hoped to create a socialist society in Afghanistan, unlike their extremist partner they sought to achieve this gradually via reforms while attempting to preserve stability and calm in the country (a position, not coincidentally, that was not in keeping with the goals and interests of the USSR).

A short time after its inception, the new establishment led by Taraki initiated a system of far-reaching reforms with a view to turning Afghanistan into a socialist state.[7]

For the regime, agrarian reform was of key socio-economic significance because the majority of the Afghan population earned its livelihood through agriculture (87% as of 1978).

The revolutionary council's "On the Land" directive of November 30, 1978, determined that there would be uncompensated expropriation of remaining lands to the state and free distribution of land to landless farmers and nomads.

Practical implementation of the reforms began on January 1, 1979, in ten of the country's provinces.

Until the April 1978 revolution, 76% of Afghanistan's population were landless and worked agricultural fields owned by others (feudal landowners).

During implementation of the reforms, a total of 740,000 dunams of land were expropriated from 35,000 landowners without compensation.

However, the reform was too extreme and ignored the social structure and traditions of Afghan society.

Farmers who were given land could not cultivate it for lack of money, seeds and tools. Many farmers refused to accept the land because they believed the land had been distributed by Allah and neither man nor government had the right to question his decisions. Moreover, community and tribal divisions and hierarchy prevented them from being able to effectively implement the land redistribution. Further, the expropriation and redistribution process was accompanied by extensive corruption.

Agrarian reform not only failed to ingratiate the government with the agricultural population but severely damaged the traditional economic system, worsened the farmers' situation and increased distrust and hostility toward the government.

In the religious sphere, despite the revolutionary council's declaration in April 1978 that the revolution in Afghanistan had been in the name of "preserving the principles of Islam and democracy," in practice the revolutionary council made a number of moves that were intended to advance democracy but offended highly sensitive religious elements and aroused strong resistance from the religious leadership. Consequently, the government took various steps to supervise and restrict the power of religious leaders.

The "Muslim Brotherhood" was declared an enemy of the state and banned. Religious leaders who opposed the government were arrested and some were publicly executed.

Throughout the country Islamic educational institutions were closed and Soviet-style socialist indoctrination was introduced in the schools.

The government's anti-religious moves resulted in mass popular resistance to the regime, and were among the primary reasons for the growth of the Mujahidin resistance movements and ensuing civil war.

The extreme reforms soon generated widespread agitation throughout the country and a worsening of the internal conflict in the highest ranks of the regime between the Khalq and the Parcham. In the developing power struggles within the administration the Khalq had the advantage and in June 1978 the leaders of the Parcham were exiled. Babrak Karmal "agreed" to serve as ambassador to Czechoslovakia. Other central Parcham figures were also appointed ambassadors in various places throughout the world. Charges of conspiring against the state were brought against leaders of the movement who decided to remain in Afghanistan and they were sentenced to long imprisonments. After neutralizing the Parcham's power, Taraki and Amin's government initiated intensified implementation of the reform plan (especially after the appointment of Amin, who was the driving force behind the reforms, as prime minister in March 1978).

On December 5, 1978, Taraki signed a "friendship agreement" with the USSR. In paragraph 4, the following was stated: "the above intended sides, acting in the spirit of the UN charter, will undertake consultations and, with the agreement of both sides, take appropriate steps to ensure security, independence and territorial integrity of the two countries. In the interests of strengthening the defensive capabilities of the above intended sides, they will continue to develop military cooperation on the basis of signed suitable agreements".[8]

This paragraph later became the legal basis for legitimization of the Soviet invasion of Afghanistan.

In the following months the conflict between the regime and its opponents grew more severe, especially in rural areas. In mid 1979 there were extensive desertions from the Afghan army, opposition activities increased and opposition forces took control of a number of regional cities. Many Soviet consultants were injured in these battles, which increased the USSR's concern about the deterioration of the internal situation on its southern border. In September 1979, Taraki visited the USSR (upon his return from the convention of non-aligned states) and the Soviets instructed him to slow down the rate of reform, depose Amin who was the driving force behind it, and try to reinstate peace and stability in the country.

Hafizullah Amin, who correctly assessed the intentions of the Soviets and Taraki, acted quickly.

On September 16, 1979, Amin declared that Taraki had been forced to resign from public activity because of health problems and that he would be taking his place (today it is clear that around this time Taraki was assassinated on Amin's orders). Despite these steps, however, in the following three months the internal situation worsened under Amin's rule.

Disquiet and agitation in Afghanistan were a source of concern for the Soviets since the spread of the Islamic-natured uprising in Afghanistan could well affect what was happening in the Muslim republics in the southern USSR, especially given the Islamic awakening simultaneously taking place in neighboring Iran.

The regime in Kabul, despite differences of opinion with the leaders in the Kremlin, was a socialist regime. Its fall in all likelihood would damage the status of the USSR. Moreover, there was concern that the regime that replaced it would be pro-Western or pro-Chinese.

The Soviets, therefore, did everything in their power to stabilize the situation in Afghanistan by means of influence and massive aid, including supply of arms, dispatch of military consultants, KGB aid in establishing the Afghan secret police and extensive economic assistance.

Mark Heller claims that, according to the chair of the Afghan Islamic League, official Soviet representatives approached the league with a proposal to expel Taraki and establish "a national unity government of only a few Communist Afghans from the ranks of the Parcham".[9] It is unclear whether this was a concrete proposal or a suggestion intended to weaken and create division in the opposition ranks. In any event, the opposition rejected this proposal believing that it could seize power itself before the winter of 1980.

After all its attempts to return order to Afghanistan through the existing regime failed, the USSR decided to act directly to change the situation.

Brezhnev justified the Soviet intervention saying there was "danger to the country's independence that could become an imperialist bridgehead on our southern border...and therefore we could not refuse the urgent request for aid from the government of Afghanistan. If we had acted otherwise it would have fallen victim to imperialist scheming. We could not remain passive in the light of the danger that had developed on our southern border".[10]

In accordance with the "Brezhnev doctrine," the USSR was obligated to do all in its power to prevent the opposition from taking over regimes friendly to the USSR. (This policy had been tested in Prague in 1968.)

The importance of keeping the Kabul regime from falling into the hands of the Islamic opposition became even more pressing in light of the success of Khomeini's Islamic revolution in neighboring Iran and the awakening of radical Islamic streams throughout the world, including among Muslim populations in the USSR.

It seems that the Kremlin's leaders also feared infiltration of Chinese influence into Afghanistan in light of information about Chinese aid given to the Afghan resistance movements at that time.[11]

Likewise, the Soviets apparently feared its move would arouse opposition from the USA and the West since it would be creating a precedent for Soviet invasion of a state that, although perceived as an ally, was not a party to the Warsaw Treaty, unlike earlier cases such as Hungary 1956 and Czechoslovakia in 1968.

The Soviet invasion of Afghanistan was a complex and carefully planned military operation that began in 1979. The main problems facing the Soviet planners were, first and foremost, how to overcome possible resistance from the Afghan army and to prepare for the possibility of Chinese military activity on the Chinese-Afghanistan border.

The Soviets were aided in formulating the campaign by a team of consultants and instructors who had served in a variety of capacities in the Afghan army.

In 1979, 4000 Soviet military personnel who had been included in the upper echelons of the Afghan command were serving in Afghanistan, in most of the decision making centers and central bases of the Afghan airforce in Kabul and Bagram.

Between December 24 and 27, 1979, a Soviet division (some 8000 soldiers and their equipment) was flown to the airports of Kabul and Bagram. Five Soviet divisions simultaneously crossed the border into Afghanistan by land and advanced towards the capital city.

On the evening of December 27, 1979, airborne Soviet forces that had landed in Kabul a few days earlier began, after heavy battles, to seize key positions, including the broadcasting station, government buildings and other central facilities.

Hafizullah Amin, who had viewed the arrival of the Soviet forces in the days leading up to the campaign as part of activity intended to aid him in his struggle against the rebels, understood the real goal that evening. Soviet paratroopers storming the presidential palace outside the city that evening destroyed the Afghan artillery unit which was defending Amin, and he was executed together with most members of his family.

In conjunction with carrying out the military coup and capturing Kabul, some five Soviet divisions began taking over the country. Heliborne forces took control of key areas in central cities, and the artillery helped to establish a hold of pivotal territories.

Three days later, Radio Kabul announced that Hafizullah Amin had been convicted of crimes against the state and was executed on the orders of the revolutionary court; Babrak Karmal, who had returned at the Soviet's initiative from Prague, was declared the new president of Afghanistan.[12]

Thus began the USSR's direct involvement in Afghanistan, which lasted close to ten years and ended with the fall of the pro-Soviet regime in 1992 (two years after the withdrawal of Soviet troops from Afghanistan).

Against the background of the country's domestic struggle between the Communist regime and the Islamic opposition, direct Soviet involvement in Afghanistan added the dimension of a national liberation war against a foreign conqueror – or, in accordance with the Islamic world view, a Jihad (holy war) for the liberation of Afghanistan from infidel rule and foreign conquest.[13]

The Soviet Invasion and the Karmal Government

After the Soviet invasion of Afghanistan a new administration was established, with Soviet aid, which set its sights on stabilizing the internal situation in the country while stressing preservation of the foundations of Islam and tribal ethnic tradition.

New basic principles were formulated into a new constitution which was published and approved by the revolutionary council on April 14, 1980.

Tens of organizations and associations of professional, religious, ethnic and tribal sectors were established in the course of 1980 in the spirit of the new constitution. This policy gave rise to the establishment in June 1980 of the High Council of Afghan Tribes and on June 15 the "National Homeland Front" was established which incorporated all the associations and organizations under the leadership of the ruling party.

The move was accompanied by a series of changes in the system of government with the revolutionary council being expanded and some of its authority transferred to various ministers. A new Prime Minister was appointed, but Karmal continued to hold the real center of power in his capacity as chair of the revolutionary council and the general secretary of the ruling party – the People's Democratic Party of Afghanistan.

Along with these political steps, agrarian reform activity declared by the previous administration was significantly suspended and various concessions were made to facilitate expansion of private agriculture and private enterprise.

The steps taken by Karmal's administration were meant to increase support for and identification with the regime in Kabul at the expense of "ideological compromises" and the introduction of traces of democracy, but this proved inadequate given the basic problems confronting the regime:[1]

1. A divided and conflict-ridden political system
2. A severe economic crisis
3. A confusing, corrupt and inefficient system of government
4. Weakened security and military forces as a result of "purges", desertions and a lack of willingness of the young to enlist in the army (the military force decreased from 90,000 individuals in 1978 to 35,000 in 1981).

The regime's weakness was especially visible in the worsening civil war and the rising pressure of the Mujahidin, which necessitated increasing involvement of Soviet forces to preserve Karmal's rule in Kabul. The extent of Soviet forces in Afghanistan grew from 85,000 individuals in 1981 to 130,000 in 1985.[2]

The Mujahidin movements, which until 1979 were disorganized and had limited military equipment and training, developed into large organized movements within Afghanistan and in refugee camps in Iran and Pakistan. The Soviet invasion introduced the dimension of an inter-bloc struggle to the internal Afghan conflict and the USA and China increased their financial and military aid to the Mujahidin movements.

The struggle between the Mujahidin and the regime in Kabul and its Soviet supporters soon turned into a religious conflict and a Jihad against the Soviets and the regime in Kabul. Volunteers from throughout the Muslim world joined and financial and military aid flowed to Mujahidin camps in Pakistan, mainly from Saudi Arabia and the Gulf States.

Revolutionary Iran under Khomeini's rule (1979) provided financial and military aid to the Shiite organizations, some of which had adopted the Khomeni ideology and worked toward importing the Iranian revolution into Afghanistan.

In the wake of these processes, the effectiveness of the Mujahidin's guerilla activities increased progressively. The government in Kabul, and especially Soviet forces, were forced to expand and deepen their involvement in fighting using increasingly more advanced weapons that the Soviets had at their disposal such as heavy bombers, fighter helicopters, scatter mines, etc.

Expansive Soviet attacks on the ground and from the air, in an attempt to purge areas under Mujahidin control and block routes of infiltration from Pakistan, seriously damaged Afghanistan's economic infrastructure and civilian population.

Serious blows to agricultural regions caused hunger and mass exodus, mainly to Pakistan which was deluged with 3 million refugees and Iran, which took in 1.5 million.

The Soviet inability to conclude the war in Afghanistan, the financial burden of the war on the Soviet economy ($10-15 million per day), the many casualties and international pressure, caused the Soviets to try to find a solution to the Afghan problem.

In February 1985 Michael Gorbachev came to power in the USSR. At a Politburo convention that same year, Gorbachev stated the need to find a "way out" of the situation. At the time, his intention was to find a "way out" via a military victory that would facilitate withdrawal of the troops and leave Afghanistan in the hands of a stable pro-Soviet Afghan regime. (Despite the above, it may be that already by 1985 there were factions in the Politburo who felt that Soviet forces should be withdrawn from Afghanistan in any event.)

At any rate, a new commander was appointed for the Soviet military forces in Afghanistan – General Michael Zeichev – who launched a broad attack on the Mujahidin in an attempt to force a conclusion.[3]

Simultaneous to the military moves, the feeling developed in the USSR that Karmal's regime was incapable of making significant achievements towards stabilizing the political situation in Afghanistan and that policy should be changed to bring about unification and cooperation of rival factions in the government.

Under Soviet pressure Karmal was forced to declare a series of changes and reforms in the governmental system, including the integration of non-Marxist elements into the revolutionary council and assignment of positions to moderate Islamists and ministerial portfolios to members of the Khalq.[4] These changes however, did not seem to spark the desired change in the status of Karmal's regime and the Soviets decided to act to "create" a new leader who could attain significant achievements in Afghan politics.

The Politburo gave the task of consolidating a new administration in Afghanistan to the KGB, the body that was closest and had the most access to what was going on in Afghanistan. Yuri Andropov (the head of the KGB at the time) chose his protege Najib, the head of the secret police in Afghanistan, as the candidate for rule in Kabul.

Following this decision Karmal was forced to acquiesce to Najib's rapid promotion in the Afghan political system. In April 1985, Najib was appointed secretary of the central committee of the ruling party, a position which he held for only five months, after which he was appointed general secretary of the party. This appointment clarified to Karmal that he was no longer regarded favorably by his patrons in the USSR and that his political fate had been sealed. In the four months that followed he still attempted a series of steps to reinforce his position but his political power continued to fade and in April 1986 Najib replaced him.

The Government of Najib (Najibullah)

The Soviet choice of Najib as Karmal's successor was not incidental, since the secret services and their leader were among the strongest, most loyal and effective elements in the higher echelons of Afghan rule that the Soviets had at their disposal.

In April 1986 Karmal was deposed in a constitutional move and his place was taken by Najib. At the end of 1986, Najib undertook a series of actions intended to strengthen his rule, including new appointments of his followers to key governmental positions and the central committee.[1]

Najib's appointment not only failed to unify the ranks and strengthen the regime's status, but actually exacerbated differences of opinion in the ruling party between members of the Parcham and Khalq and even within the ranks of the Parcham between supporters of Karmal and supporters of Najib.

In December 1986 Najib was invited to visit Moscow in a gesture intended to demonstrate Soviet support for his regime. At that stage, however, its appears that Moscow had already decided on gradual withdrawal of its forces from Afghanistan. The aim of the visit was to prepare the ground for withdrawal, an action which would be "painful and dangerous" for the Afghan regime.

During the visit, the Soviets and the regime in Kabul apparently formulated a new policy to bring about a cease-fire and national reconciliation in Afghanistan. In January 1987 a first step was taken in this direction when the Afghan government called for a 6-month cease-fire and the establishment of a national reconciliation government. Both initiatives were rejected by the Mujahidin movements, who stepped up their attacks. Soviet attacks on the

Mujahidin were also increased and cease-fires declared in July 1987 and January 1988 were not implemented in practice.

In April 1988 the Geneva Accords signed (with the patronage of the superpowers) between Afghanistan and Pakistan were meant to regulate involvement of the superpowers (USSR and USA) in the Afghan conflict, with the USSR undertaking to evacuate half of its forces by August 15, 1988.[2]

In the ensuing months, Najib's government made repeated attempts to enter into dialogue with the Mujahidin movements while performing a number of gestures such as prisoner release, among them members of the Khalq,[3] and allocation of $40 million to religious causes (appointment of 846 Islamic clergy in the police and military), despite the fact that support of religion was fundamentally in conflict with Najib's Marxist world view.[4]

At the same time, steps were taken toward political change: a new and more liberal party law was passed, a new constitution came into effect and a national assembly with broader representation of non-Communist elements was established.

In the economic field, private investments were permitted and even encouraged by means of generous loans and low interest rates. In November Najib declared that there would be land distribution reform (agrarian reform would be frozen), and land ownership by individuals and companies would be permitted.[5]

Najib promised that any village that declared its allegiance to the regime in Kabul would (even without proving it in practice) not be harmed by shelling or aerial bombing by government forces.

On the symbolic level the country's name was changed from the Afghan Democratic Republic (a name with Communist connotations) to the Afghan Republic and **Najib himself adopted a variation of his name to one having more Islamic associations – Najibullah.**

In the military area, Najib doubled the salaries of military personnel, gave promotions and benefits to senior commanders and increased the rate of enlistment in the army (in practice this was implemented only in Kabul), but these steps did not improve his military capabilities.[6]

The Mujahidin movements, knowing that Soviet withdrawal from Afghanistan was near, estimated that they could vanquish the regime in Kabul when it was on its own and therefore refused to comply with Najibullah's conciliatory efforts.

Moreover, while diplomatic contacts continued under the patronage of the UN and the superpowers, battles initiated by the Mujahidin grew more fierce. The Soviets responded with heavy air bombardment that left a "scorched earth" behind them and deepened the hatred and lack of trust of the majority of the Afghan population against Najibullah's regime.

The Fall of Najibullah's Regime and the Rise of the Mujahidin

Agreements between the USA and the USSR under Gorbachev regarding withdrawal of the Soviet forces from Afghanistan (February 15, 1992), cessation of American military aid to the Mujahidin and UN activities toward achieving peace agreements left Najibullah's regime isolated in the conflict against the Mujahidin.

At first Najibullah believed he could withstand the Mujahidin whose progress toward conquering strategic power centers in the country had been slowed by internal rivalries. He therefore adopted an uncompromising line in the negotiations that took place under UN patronage.

A UN delegation began mainly humanitarian work on the Pakistan-Afghanistan border on April 1988. After the Soviet withdrawal from Afghanistan, UN missions were expanded and a mediator sent by the Secretary General Benon Sevan began attempts to mediate between the Mujahidin and the regime in Kabul in 1992.

The UN's compromise proposal was to establish a temporary "ruling council" that would include representatives of all the Mujahidin movements and of Najibullah's regime and would serve until the situation in the country stabilized and general elections could be held. Najibullah rejected the proposed compromise in hopes of deepening the rifts in the ranks of the Mujahidin and reaching an agreement with some of the Mujahidin to ensure the survival of his regime. Simultaneously, discussions between factions of the Mujahidin to formulate a coordinated policy and fight Najibullah's regime were also underway.

On October 27, 1991, the Islamabad agreement was signed in which the Mujahidin movements agreed to the following:

1. Vociferous demand for the deposition of Najibullah.
2. Closer ties between Mujahidin field commanders and leaders of the relevant movements of the Islamic Union in Afghanistan.
3. A call for immediate elections in 13 northern provinces of Afghanistan even before the temporary ruling council was established.

On March 18, 1992, after heavy pressure from President Yeltsin, Najibullah declared in a speech to the Afghan nation that he and his government would resign when a neutral transitional government representing all elements of Afghan society would be able to undertake temporary rule.

Boutrous Ali (General Secretary of the UN) simultaneously announced that a temporary transitional council with 15 members would take charge in Kabul on April 28, 1992.

On April 16, 1992, Najibullah suddenly disappeared from public view. It seems he tried to flee Kabul but failed and took refuge in a UN facility in Kabul.

Abed El Rahman Hatef, one of Najibullah's four deputies, was temporarily appointed acting president and went to the north of the country to meet with Sheikh Ahmed Masud, one of the leaders of the Mujahidin. The Mujahidin rejected this initiative however and continued to advance toward Kabul.

On April 17, the city of Gardeyz was taken by Hekmatyar's forces while the city of Herat in the west fell into the hands of Mujahidin led by Ismail Khan. The rapid collapse of the Najibullah regime found the Mujahidin organizations divided, in conflict with one another and with no consolidated plans for positing an alternative to the Marxist regime that had crumbled.[1]

The first to reach the capital of Kabul were the forces of Sheikh Ahmed Masud, military commander of the Islamic Jamiat movement headed by Burhanuddin Rabbani. The conquest of the city was almost bloodless because most of the forces of the old regime had either fled or defected to the Mujahidin side (for example General Dostum's forces). A short while after Sheikh Masud's forces entered the capital, heavy battles broke out between them and rival militias headed by Hekmatyar, head of the Islamic party (Hizb-e-Islami).

After three rounds of battle, during which various parts of the city transferred from hand to hand, between the forces of Sheikh Masud and a coalition of the Islamic Party and the union of pro-Iranian Shiite militias (Hizbi-e-Wahadat, a union of seven pro-Iranian Shiite parties), Masud prevailed and his rivals withdrew from Kabul.[2]

On April 24, 1992, under the patronage of the UN, an agreement was signed at Peshawar between five Mujahidin movement leaders to establish a temporary ruling council for a two-month period led by a compromise candidate, Sibghatullah Mujaddedi, head of the National Liberation Front.

Despite the military victory of the Jamaat e Islami movement and its control of Kabul, Rabbani and Masud, the heads of the movement, understood that they would not be able to institute a stable regime based on their movement alone, which represented mainly the Tajiki minority. They therefore decided to honor the agreement. But Hekmatyar and his allies continued their violent struggle against the Jamaat e Islami in Kabul and other provinces.

Members of the council headed by Sibghatullah Mujaddedi came to Kabul on April 28, 1992, and formally received control from representatives of Najibullah's regime. During the ceremony Mujaddedi declared the establishment of the "Islamic Republic of Afghanistan," granted general amnesty to all who had worked for Najibullah's regime and called on workers to a return to work to renew essential services for the city's population. Only Najibullah was not included in the declaration of amnesty.[3]

In Mujaddedi's first public appearance as head of the temporary ruling council in Kabul on May 1, 1992, he declared that the war was over and that forces should join together to build the country. He called to Hekmatyar to join the government as prime minister but demanded that his followers surrender their arms before entering Kabul.

Hekmatyar responded to Mujaddedi's proposals on April 4 with heavy bombardment of Kabul, resulting in many casualties.

On May 5, 1992, Mujaddedi announced the establishment of a 35-member cabinet in which most Mujahidin factions were represented. (Vacant seats in the cabinet were saved for movements that had not yet joined, hoping that they would do so in future.)

Ahmad Sayed Gailani, head of the National Islamic Front of Afghanistan, was appointed foreign minister. Abdul Rasul Sayyaf, head of the Islamic Unity of Afghan Mujahidin movements, was appointed minister of the interior. Abed el Haq, commander of the Kabul region Mujahidin, was appointed minister of police, and Sheikh Ahmed Masud was appointed minister of defense.

Kabul rapidly changed from a secular city where alcohol and drugs were available and women wore Western clothes to a religiously observant city run according to the strict rules of Islam (Shariah). Alcohol, prostitution and drugs were banned, women were required to wear traditional dress and ministers and government officials exchanged their suits for traditional Afghan costume.

A short time after the temporary ruling council was consolidated Mujaddedi tried to change the political "rules of the game," dropped the word **temporary** from the name of the ruling council and declared his intention to remain in power for two years.

The leaders of the Jamaat e Islami were not reconciled with Mujaddedi's intentions and in June 1992 he was deposed. A new government under Burhanuddin Rabbani as president was established, with Sheikh Ahmed Masud as minister of defense.[4] The government was based on a relatively broad coalition of Mujahidin and other movements, but the major centers of power and influence were retained by the Jamaat e Islami, made up of minority Tajiki members.[5]

Afghanistan – Islamic Opposition and the Mujahidin Movements

The Jihad against the secular regime of Amanallah Khan who had tried to implement western style reforms in the 1920s and the Anglo-Afghan wars (also called Jihad) were the historical cornerstones and model of inspiration to be copied in the Mujahidin's struggle against Kabul's Marxist regime and the Soviet forces that assisted it from the 1970s onwards.

In this struggle, outside forces had a major influence on the development of the society and regime in Afghanistan.

The USSR's attempts to consolidate a Communist regime in Afghanistan, first through aid and indirect involvement and later through direct military involvement, were major components in the development of the civil war in Afghanistan which eventually led to the victory of the Mujahidin and the rise of the fundamentalist Islamic regime.

Soviet involvement in Afghanistan must be analyzed not only from the point of view of a struggle over influential regions and the Soviet fear of threat to its southern border from infiltration of Western influences, but also as an intercultural conflict.

In his book "The Clash of Civilizations and the Remaking of World Order",[1] Professor Huntington maintains that the war between the USSR and the Mujahidin in Afghanistan is one aspect of the conflict between Western European culture represented by the USSR and Islamic culture. (Huntington includes the USSR in his definition of Western culture without addressing the ideological differences between socialism and liberalism in a bi-polar system.)

The Afghan Mujahidin waged their struggle against the USSR not only as a national liberation war but as a Jihad in which radical Islamic elements from throughout the Muslim world took part and which had the blessing of most Arab and Muslim states.

From a Soviet perspective, the war in Afghanistan was necessary not only to prevent the fall of a pro-Soviet regime, but also out of fear that the rise of a radical Islamic regime in Afghanistan would endanger stability in the USSR's Muslim republics.

These fears were reinforced by the rise to power of Khomeini in Iran in 1979 and the wave of radicalism that swept the Muslim world.

The Soviet response to the threat was its invasion of Afghanistan to protect the incumbent pro-Soviet regime, and its support of the Iraqi regime that launched a war on Khomeini's Iran (September 1980).

The slogan of radical Islam, "neither East nor West," was implemented in full in two neighboring Muslim countries when Khomeini defeated the American-supported Shah and expelled his Western influence from Iran and Afghanistan almost simultaneously began a Jihad against Soviet presence and influence.

The Soviets correctly gauged the significance of the rise of an extremist Islamic regime in Afghanistan. Their failure in the war against Afghanistan and the subsequent collapse of the USSR made tangible the Islamic threat to the Muslim Republics that emerged from the ruins of the USSR.

Afghanistan's neighbors Iran (already mentioned) and especially Pakistan, were also seriously influenced by their involvement with and support of the Mujahidin in the conflict against Kabul's Marxist regime and by their ties to ethnic groups in Afghanistan (in Pakistan amongst the Pashtun population which forms the majority in Afghanistan and in Iran amongst Shiite populations). This is in addition to the political, national and regional interests of these countries.

The attempt to form a Soviet style socialist state in Afghanistan was accompanied by a rapid and acute process of modernization. Traditional tribal Afghan society with its Islamic orientation was not ready for the changes that the central regime in Kabul wanted to impose. An identity crisis ensued which was expressed by vehement resistance to reform, a process, incidentally, characteristic of many Muslim societies. But because of unique components of Afghan society (as a tribally and ethnically divided society), this process resulted in particularly severe consequences.

Other important components characterizing the Afghan arena were religious conflict between the secular Marxist regime and the majority of traditional and tribally-oriented Afghan Muslims, and rivalry amongst ethnic groups. In light of the above, the Marxist regime in Kabul failed to obtain legitimization from significant parts of the population who set out to struggle against it. Moreover, socialist secular elements were also divided amongst themselves (the Parcham against the Khalq). The governments that arose in Kabul had extremely limited legitimization, and they depended mainly on the loyalty of security forces and support from the USSR (which shows once again the importance of and dependence on an outside element).

On the economic level, the central government in Kabul tried, before the outbreak of the civil war, to implement far-reaching changes in the spirit of socialism by undertaking agrarian reform, industrialization and attempts to dismantle and change the traditional agricultural economy based on feudal and tribal distribution.

Attempts to implement reform led to intensified urbanization and the development of poverty centers in and around large urban areas, especially Kabul, as well as damaged the already delicate and insecure fabric of the Afghan economy. The years of the civil war brought almost total paralysis to the economy and destroyed significant portions of the country's economic infrastructure.

The regime in Kabul was dictatorial in nature and relied on intelligence services, the army and, especially, on a massive Soviet military presence.

The regime was based on laws and enforcement methods intended to ensure its survival. Its influence was mainly in the capital Kabul and provincial cities while, in the periphery, the traditional decentralization and a large measure of autonomy continued. The military weakness of the Kabul regime necessitated increased Soviet involvement over the civil war years, but military aid received by the Mujahidin organizations from Muslim countries and the USA enabled them to compete with increasing success against the Soviet forces in Afghanistan.

The withdrawal of Soviet forces from Afghanistan sealed the fate of the pro-Soviet regime. It survived an additional two years mainly because of internal power struggles within the ranks of the Mujahidin, which delayed coordination of efforts to destroy it. The Mujahidin movements were characterized throughout the years of the struggle against the regime in Kabul and the Soviet forces by division and (sometimes violent) power struggles that impaired their ability to coordinate the struggle against the common enemy.

There was no charismatic leader among the Afghan Mujahidin able to unify the ranks. Military and political leaders emerged from the various movements, but no effective umbrella framework acceptable to all the movements developed.

It seems this reality resulted from the tradition, history and ethnic composition of the Afghan population which, despite long years of war against a common enemy, not only failed to close ranks, but grew even more divided.

The fall of the Marxist regime in Kabul in 1992, therefore, found the Mujahidin movements split and unready to act as an orderly alternative to the regime.

The Afghan Mujahidin Movements

Throughout the war in Afghanistan, the name Mujahidin or "resistance" movements referred to the opposition that battled against the Marxist regime and its Soviet allies.

Influenced by the "Muslim Brotherhood," Islamic fundamentalist groups began to form in Afghanistan as early as the mid-1950s as a counterbalance to the growth of democratic and socialist political movements.

These groups aspired to the establishment of a state and regime in the spirit of the foundations of Shariah and the Koran and the expulsion of foreign influences from Afghanistan. In the mid 1960s the Faculty of Theology at Kabul University became one of the most important centers for Islamic political and underground activity.

Under the patronage of the dean of the Faculty of Theology Professor Naizi, an extremist Islamic group comprised of students and lecturers from the Naizi faculty was established.

Simultaneously, another extremist Islamic group was formed in the Faculty of Engineering under the leadership of Gulbuddin Hekmatyar, Suffudin Naftyar and Habib Rahman. Burhanuddin Rabbani, one of the leaders of the "Muslim Brotherhood" in Kabul, mediated the consolidation of the two groups and the first fundamentalist Islamic movement in Afghanistan – "The Muslim Youth League" – was established. The organization was presided over by a high council composed of the founders: Niazi, Rabbani, Tabaneh, Sayyaf, Hekmatyar and Naftayar.

From its inception, the Muslim Youth League adopted an extremist ideology that advocated conflict with the secular establishment in Afghanistan.

After the rise to power of Mohammed Daoud and the policies of reform he tried to implement, the organization became divided. The extremist faction led by Hekmatyar demanded launching an armed struggle to overthrow Daoud and establish an Islamic state while the moderate faction aspired to reinstate the monarchy and effect a more moderate traditional Islamic rule.

In 1973 the radical faction led by Hekmatyar began engaging in insurrection and terror against Daoud's regime but government forces managed to suppress the uprising. Many of the movement's members were arrested, executed or fled to neighboring Pakistan.

From the latter half of the 1970s, and increasingly after the USSR invasion of Afghanistan, protest and resistance expanded.

The Afghan opposition was characterized by heterogeneity of its components resulting from ethnic, religious (Sunni/Shiite), political and ideological differences, and by the absence of a central authoritative and purposeful leadership.[2]

The only common denominator among the groups and organizations was the desire to banish the Marxist regime that ruled in Kabul and the Soviet invading forces. However, this common aim was not sufficient to prevent rivalries and violent power struggles between the various factions which sometimes exposed them to serious blows from their common enemy (the regime and the Soviet forces).

Most of the Mujahidin movements centered around traditional religious leadership based on ethnic and regional considerations, although some of the movements were heterogeneous and included supporters and activists from various ethnic groups.

The protest movement formed around local political and religious leaders and gradually developed into two main factions.

The first faction adopted principles from the ideology of the Muslim Brotherhood and advocated Jihad against the Communist regime with a view to transforming Afghanistan into an Islamic state in the spirit of Islamic law (Shariah). This stream became known as the "fundamentalist stream."

The second faction also advocated struggle against the Communist regime, but its aim was to found a regime in the unique tribal tradition of Afghanistan. A significant portion of the leaders of this faction came from the ranks of the supporters of King Zahir and inspired to reinstate the monarchy. This stream, which became known as the "traditional" or "moderate" stream, felt that the life of the individual should be guided by Islam but community and state problems should be solved in the "tribal Afghan way".[3]

The Mujahidin movements which grew and consolidated from the two streams in Afghanistan during the war against the Marxist regime in Kabul faithfully reflect the heterogeneity and complexity of Afghan society. There are twelve main Mujahidin movements (along with tens of militias and local organizations, the discussion of which lies beyond the scope of this book).

These movements are characterized by countless divisions and rifts, based mainly on the personal and tribal rivalries of their leaders. Therefore, while the number of movements is outstanding, there are few significant differences among them. (Furthermore, some of the organizations kept their original names even after splitting. See Hizb-e-Islami).

Sunni Organizations

1. Jamaat-e-Islami – The Islamic Movement of Afghanistan
Leader – Burhanuddin Rabbani
An Islamic fundamentalist-oriented movement advocating the foundation of a theocratic republic. Most members of this movement are of Tajiki extraction.

2. Hizb-e-Islami – The Islamic Party
Leader – Gulbuddin Hekmatyar
An extremist Islamic-oriented movement advocating the foundation of a central Islamic republic. Most members are Pashtun. The organization is at variance and in conflict with the majority of the other Islamic movements.

3. Hizb-e-Islami – The Islamic Party
Leader – Younis Khalis
A fundamentalist-oriented movement that advocates the foundation of a theocratic republic. Most of its members are Pashtun (on a tribal basis).

4. The Islamic Alliance of Afghan Mujahidin
Leader – Abdul Rasul Sayyaf
An organization with a conservative ideology that advocates the establishment of an Islamic republic. The organization developed into a body that attempted to unify various Afghan elements located in Pakistan.

5. The Islamic National Front of Afghanistan
Leader – Pir Sayed Ahmad Gailani
A monarchist organization that aligns itself with reinstatement of the monarchy (in the pre-revolutionary format). Most members are Pashtun.

6. (Harakat-e-Inquilab Islami) – The Islamic Revolutionary Movement
Leader – Mohammed Nabi Mohammedi
A conservative organization that aligns itself with returning to the pre-revolutionary establishment (a relatively moderate organization). Most of its members are Pashtun.

7. The National Liberation Front
Leader – Sibghatullah Mujaddedi
A monarchist organization that supports reestablishment of the Pashtun establishment in the pre-revolutionary format. This is a relatively small organization among the Pashtun population.

Shiite Organizations in Afghanistan

Afghanistan's Shiite/Hazara population is concentrated mainly in three mountainous provinces in the Hazarajat region in the west of the country. It numbers approximately 1.5 million inhabitants.

The minority Shiite areas were amongst the most weakened by prolonged discrimination in the allocation of development resources by the central government in Kabul. Shiites in western Afghanistan were therefore among the first to rise up against the central regime in Kabul in 1978-1979.[4]

A popular uprising developed in the Shiite areas during these years. Government officials from Kabul who governed there were murdered or banished. A local Shiite administration called "the Revolutionary Council of the Islamic Union of Afghanistan" or "Shura" for short, was established. Its leader was Sayed Ali Beheshti.

The movement included a civil system that handled education, health and all other civil matters, a military wing, and liaison and publicity offices that operated from Iran and Pakistan. The Shura was the largest Shiite movement in Afghanistan and controlled 60% of the territories inhabited by Shiites, but was weakened by internal divisions and rifts.

The second most important movement was the Nasser (victory) movement, which was pro-Khomeini-Iranian. In 1980-1982 a rupture occurred between the leadership of this movement and Iran because the former demonstrated excessive independence and deviated from the Iranian political line. As a result, Iran shifted its support to other organizations such as the "Hizbullah" and the Revolutionary Guards.

Main Shiite organizations:

1. Shura
Leader – Sayed Ali Beheshti
The organization advocates establishment of a Hazara autonomy. It reached its height of power in 1979-1980 but later lost Iranian support to more radical Shiite organizations.

2. Nasser – Victory
Leader – Mir Hussein Tsadiki
An organization that advocates Hazara separatism. The organization was

supported in the early 1980s by the Iranians as a counterbalance to the Shura but gradually became "overly independent" and lost Iran's support.

3. Harkat-e-Islami – Movement of Islami Revolution
Leader – Mohammed Alsayyaf Muhseini
The organization advocates establishment of an Islamic state. It was supported by the Hazara population and the Dari-speaking Shiite populations.

4. The Revolutionary Guards
Leader – Muhsein Razzai
A Khomeini-Hazara organization that advocates unification with Iran. Since 1984 the organization has received massive Iranian support.

5. Hizbullah
Leader – unknown
A Hazara organization with a Khomeini orientation that advocates unification with Iran. The organization receives substantial support from Iran and maintains cooperative ties with Hizbullah in other countries.

Afghan Mujahidin organizations can be classified according to a number of criteria:
- **The religious component** – Of 12 movements, seven are based on Sunni leadership and support, while five are identified as Shiite movements.
  In general the Shiite movements received support from Iran while the Sunni organizations were supported mainly by Pakistan, Saudi Arabia and the USA. There are, however, examples of Iranian support for radical groups among Sunni movements, such as Hekmatyar.
- **The ethnic component** – Six of the 12 movements have Pashtun majorities (all Sunni movements), one is Tajiki dominated (Rabbani's movement) and five have Shiite majorities.
- **The ideological component** – The common denominator of all the Mujahidin movements was their demand to oust the Marxist regime and the Soviet forces supporting it from Kabul by means of a holy war – Jihad – and their desire to establish a state governed by Islamic law.

Regarding the character, status, borders, and ethnic and political affiliations of that state, the movements were divided into four main groups:

- Extremist Sunni organizations
- Moderate Sunni/monarchist organizations
- Shiite organizations advocating unification with Iran
- Shiite organizations advocating Hazara separatism

From the point of view of political power, extent of support of the population and military strength, the Sunni movements were the dominant component of the Mujahidin. The Shiite movements were smaller and their influence on the political power structure of Afghanistan was secondary.[5]

The Mujahidin movements were heavily influenced by the involvement of foreign elements, which offered them financial support and arms. Thus, Iran stood behind the Shiite movements, while Pakistan, Saudi Arabia and the USA supported all the Sunni Mujahidin organizations based in the Peshawar region of Pakistan.[6]

In 1978-1979, thirty different Afghan resistance groups (Mujahidin) were active in Pakistan. The number rose as high as forty following the Soviet invasion of Afghanistan. Most, however, were small movements that split or later joined larger movements.

A number of attempts to consolidate a unified political military front were made during the war, at least by the Mujahidin movements operating from Pakistan[7]:

- In August 1979 an attempt was made by four Afghan Mujahidin movements in Pakistan to establish a coalition. The failure of this attempt was due to an inability to agree on a unified leadership for the movement.
- In March 1980, six central Mujahidin movements gathered under one umbrella organization called the Islamic Alliance for the Liberation of Afghanistan to create a unified lobby which would seek international recognition and financial and military aid. This attempt also failed.
- During 1982 a third attempt was made to form a coalition of the Afghan Mujahidin movements. Seven of the main Mujahidin movements in Peshawar gathered under one umbrella organization called the Peshawar Seven. The movements of Hekmatyar, Rabbani, Younis Khalis, Sayyaf, Mohammedi, Gailani and Mujaddedi were partners in this alliance. But this coalition was short-lived as well, due to ideological and practical conflicts of interest between the two main Mujahidin streams (the monarchists and the fundamentalists).

In mid-1983 an additional fissure occurred after which two umbrella organizations for the Afghan Mujahidin were established:[8]

- **The fundamentalist Afghan organizations** – The movements of Rabbani, Younis Khalis, Rasul Sayyaf and Hekmatyar established the Mujahidin movement for the Islamic Unification of Afghanistan. Rasul Sayyaf was appointed head of the new movement and Hekmatyar acted as deputy.

- **The traditional Afghan organizations** – The movements of Mujaddedi, Muhammedi and Gailani established the Islamic Alliance with Gailani as head.

Another example of an attempt to unify the Mujahidin movements is the Pan-Turkish Islamic movement which hoped to unify all Mujahidin movements that had the appropriate ethnic sympathies.

The movement declared its long-term ambition to be the liberation from the USSR of all territories occupied by Muslims of Turkish origin and, as its short-term aim, to topple the Marxist regime in Kabul.[9]

Despite its ambitious goals, the movement was content in practice to attempt to fashion an Islamic alternative to the Marxist government in Kabul which, at the same time, was trying to please ethnic minorities by permitting limited national expression including Turkish national expression.[10]

The fact that at the time there were no movement leaders of Turkmeni or Uzbeki origin in Peshawar did not prevent the movement's leaders and their Pakistani patrons from trying to recruit additional members.

The movement did not manage to crystallize enough to become a significant political or military factor. Its achievements were limited to the creation of patron/client relationships with a number of local Mujahidin leaders in northern Afghanistan, usually Turkmenis or Uzbekis, ex-members of the earlier Harakat-e-inquilab Islami movement.

The main Mujahidin movements in Peshawar, such as Hizb-e-Islami and Jamaat e Islami, came out strongly against the Pan-Turkish Islamic movement, blaming it for causing an ethnic rift in the ranks of the Islamic resistance and of cooperating with the Marxist regime in Kabul.

These movements claimed that the Afghan secret service made use of the Pan-Turkish Islamic movement, which was insufficiently cautious about selecting members, to infiltrate agents into the ranks of the Afghan resistance. Therefore it was a "Trojan horse" in the hands of the regime in Kabul.[11]

Be that as it may, the movement failed to achieve its aims and gradually faded until it disappeared almost entirely from the political map of Afghanistan after the Mujahidin victory over the Marxist regime in Kabul.

The moderate Sunni/monarchist movements were the weakest of the Sunni movements, but their religious and ethnic composition often enabled them to achieve politically powerful positions as catalysts of compromise and mediation between the major rivals in the Sunni camp: Hekmatyar's Hizb-e-Islami and Rabbani's Jamaat e Islami.

Leaders of the Mujahidin Movements in Afghanistan

Burhanuddin Rabbani[1]

Rabbani, a Tajiki, was born in 1940. He studied religion at Kabul University and earned a Masters degree in religious studies from Al-Azhar University in Cairo (1966). During his stay in Egypt he established an underground resistance movement against the monarchy in Afghanistan.

In 1968 he returned to Afghanistan from Egypt to teach religious studies at Kabul University. In this period he was involved in the establishment of an extremist Islamic student movement which set its sights on combating deviations from religion and corruption in the regime.

Following the rise to power of Mohammed Daoud and the foundation of the leftist regime in Afghanistan, his movement began to take action against it. A warrant for Rabbani's arrest was issued as a result of this activity and he fled from Kabul to Peshawar in Pakistan.[2]

In Peshawar, Rabbani established a Mujahidin movement that received aid from many countries including Pakistan, the Gulf states and other Arab countries, while underground cells that were the basis of a widespread guerilla movement were simultaneously established in Afghanistan.

Rabbani's movement had an Islamic orientation and advocated the establishment of an Islamic state in the spirit of Shariah. In the early years of his activism he took an extremist political line, claiming that "Russia is the first enemy and the West the second."[3] As of 1983, however, he changed his approach, moderated his criticism of the West and welcomed the Western aid necessary for his struggle against the Soviets and the Marxist regime in Kabul and the sometimes violent encounters with rival Mujahidin movements, especially the Hizb-e-Islami led by Hekmatyar.

Rabbani made it clear that he opposed the extremist militant model of Islamic states such as Khomeini's Iran and aspired to founding an Islamic state that would know how to combine modern technology with Islamic values and live in peace with other countries.[4]

During the war in Afghanistan, especially towards the end of it, his movement became the strongest among the Afghan Mujahidin and enabled him to come to power.

Gulbuddin Hekmatyar

Hekmatyar was a Pashtun (the largest ethnic group in Afghanistan). He was born in 1948 and studied engineering at Kabul University. During his studies he was involved with Rabbani and Sayyaf in the establishment of an extremist Islamic student organization.

In 1968 Hekmatyar left the student organization which was not extreme enough for his tastes and established his own organization (Hizb-e-Islami – which later became a Mujahidin movement) that was active in 1968-1973 mainly against leftist student organizations in Kabul.

In 1972 Hekmatyar murdered a left-wing student at Kabul University and went underground as a fugitive from the authorities. In 1973 he fled to Peshawar in Pakistan.

Hekmatyar based his movement in Peshawar and gradually turned it into the second largest and second most influential Afghan Mujahidin movement.

During his stay in Peshawar, Hekmatyar forged extensive ties with Pakistan, Libya, Saudi Arabia and even Iran and received broad support for his movement which amassed many successes in its struggle against the Soviets.

Hekmatyar's movement was the first to launch armed struggle against the regime in Kabul, as early as the time of Babrak Karmal.

Hekmatyar was considered the most extreme of the Afghan Mujahidin leaders. In his opinion both superpowers, the USSR and the USA, were enemies of Islam. Therefore, sooner or later after the struggle with the USSR, Islam would also have to confront the USA.[5]

Hekmatyar aspired to the establishment of a Khomeini Iranian-style Islamic state to be ruled according the laws of Shariah. In an interview, Hekmatyar said that "democracy and Islam are not compatible. Afghanistan is not an Islamic state but it will be. A group of wise people will adopt the laws of Islam, alcohol will be banned, women will stay in the home and the power will be in the hands of the Mullahs".[6]

Hekmatyar's uncompromising and extreme approach gave rise to many power struggles between him and other Mujahidin leaders when, even after the victory of the Mujahidin, Hekmatyar continued his violent struggle against Mujahidin regimes that were established in Kabul.

Mohammed Khalis Younis

Khalis was born in 1941. He graduated from religious school (Mavlavi), was a teacher of religion, a poet and the editor of a religious newspaper.

In 1977 he published a book in Kabul in which he sharply criticized Daoud's leftist regime. Following the publication he was pursued by the regime. He fled to Peshawar where he joined Hekmatyar's movement (Hizb-e-Islami).

In 1979 he left Hekmatyar's movement and established a small Mujahidin organization that also bore the name Hizb-e-Islami.

Unlike the leaders of most Mujahidin movements in Peshawar who mainly engaged in political activity, Mohammed Khalis Younis directly commanded his followers in some of their guerilla actions in Afghanistan and, thereby, earned the admiration of both his supporters and his rivals. Later he declared his affiliation with the Taliban movement.

Rasul Sayyaf

Sayyaf was born in 1940. He is a graduate of the Faculty of Religion at Kabul University and holds an MA in religious studies from Al-Azhar University in Cairo. During his studies in Cairo he joined the Muslim Brotherhood. He speaks fluent Arabic and is renowned for his good relations with Saudi Arabia.

At the end of the 1960s he returned to Afghanistan and was involved in the establishment of the Islamic student movement at Kabul University with Rabbani and Hekmatyar.

In 1975 he was arrested by Daoud's regime for political activity and jailed until 1980 when he was released by Babrak Karmal. He moved to Peshawar and there established his Mujahidin movement.

Despite the fact that his political power was relatively limited, Sayyaf was accepted by the rest of the Mujahidin leaders and elected as a compromise candidate to head the Peshawar Seven movement (an organization that tried to unite and coordinate the activities of seven radical Mujahidin movements).

In terms of ideology, Sayyaf's approach is close to Hekmatyar's and his hostility to the West is marked. Among other statements he said that "if the USA or a non-Muslim country helps us, it does so only for its own selfish reasons".[7]

Sayed Ahmad Gailani

Gailani was born in 1932 to a wealthy family of landowners whose roots and lineage reach as far back as the Prophet Mohammed.

In 1954 he finished his Islamic law studies at Kabul University. During 1965-1970 he was King Zahir's religious advisor, in which capacity he worked to adapt the laws of the state to the laws of Islam.

In 1970-1978 Gailani focused on developing his family business throughout the world and built strong ties with the Saudi royal family (he sometimes used a Saudi passport on his travels).

After the 1978 coup he was Taraki's religious advisor for a brief period, but he left Kabul because of the regime's Marxist position, moved to Peshawar and established a Mujahidin movement.

Gailani has many supporters in the Pashtun-speaking provinces because of his family connections, religious status and brothers, who were leaders of guerilla forces in those areas.

Despite his religious background Gailani seemed the most moderate and secular of the Mujahidin leaders. His appearance in Western style suits and articulate English contribute to his secular image.

Among the leaders in Peshawar Gailani had the most solid program with regard to the future character of Afghanistan after the Soviet expulsion. Gailani sought a multi-party parliamentary democracy and a mixed economy that would provide for the welfare of the individual but permit free enterprise. Likewise, Gailani maintained his connections with King Zahir and the exiled circles close to him.

Gailani refrained from taking extreme positions toward the West and welcomed aid from the USA and non-Muslim countries.

Gailani's rivals accused him of lack of leadership skills and a life of leisure at the expense of contributions intended for the Mujahidin.

Mohammed Nabi Mohammedi

Mohammedi was a religious scholar (Mavlavi) and member of parliament during the reign of King Zahir. He was known for his extreme religious opinions.

After the rise to power of Mohammed Daoud he exiled himself to Peshawar and headed a relatively small Mujahidin movement.

In 1983, to the surprise of his supporters, he joined the moderate "Triple Union" causing a rift in his movement and the desertion of the more extreme elements to the more extreme Peshawar Seven Mujahidin alliance.[8]

The movement has no clear political line and its influence in Afghanistan is relatively limited.

Sibhatullah Mujadeddi

Mujaddedi is over 70 years old and is a member of one of the aristocratic and religious families in Afghanistan. He heads the National Liberation Front movement and was the first temporary president of the Mujahidin regime in Afghanistan (April 1992). His family has close ties with the deposed King Zahir Shah and he supports the return of the king and the reinstatement of the monarchy in Afghanistan.

Military Leadership of the Mujahidin

During the war, military commanders who conducted the war against the Soviets and the Marxist regime emerged in tandem with religious/political leaders. Some of these commanders acquired fame and vast political power when, at the end of the struggle against the regime in Kabul, they were placed in central positions of political power and influence.

The Mujahidin forces usually operated on a local basis and almost never ventured beyond their residential territory. They even objected to the formulation of comprehensive strategic principles.

Repeated failure of the Mujahidin to launch widespread attacks and conquer cities reinforced the preference for operating a decentralized campaign on a tactical level and leaving execution of a coordinated comprehensive effort (strategic) to the final stage, as indeed happened in 1992.

Hence, most of the Mujahidin forces employed guerilla tactics including surprise attacks and ambushes, mainly along main transport routes and against isolated strongholds. This method of warfare required formation of a system of informants and supporters among the Hazara population, mobility and the ability to move small forces from sector to sector, to coordinate them for the performance of an attack and to disperse them afterwards to minimize their vulnerability to retaliation.

Towards the end of the civil war a forum of field commanders of Mujahidin forces was convened which began to discuss the future of the country, the struggle and their status in the future political system. Many of the Mujahidin field commanders felt that "politicians" who had remained safely in Pakistan were reaping the fruit of their struggle and pushing them into the margins of the political map.

The driving force behind the forum, called the council of Mujahidin field commanders,[1] was Sheikh Ahmed Masud, a member of the Tajiki minority. During the war, he built and consolidated one of the most organized and trained militias, at the head of which he was the first to enter Kabul in 1992.

During the war Masud kept a "low profile," stayed away from the centers of publicity and political activity in Pakistan, and preferred a Spartan way of life with his soldiers in Afghanistan.

He used these years not only to amass power, but also to recruit a broad infrastructure of supporters who provided a logistical and political home front during and after the war.

At the forum meetings on October 9-12, 1991, Masud spoke against involvement of the Pakistani intelligence services in the Mujahidin movements and claimed that the government forces could be brought to surrender by means of a siege and blockading the supply routes between the main urban centers.

Masud believed that the Mujahidins' failure in the frontal battle for Kabul would distance them from their objective for many years and enable Najibullah's regime to survive and rehabilitate itself. The majority of the Mujahidin field commanders agreed with Masud but Hekmatyar's organization was eager for action. On December 10-12, 1991, his forces independently attacked Kabul, were rebuffed by government forces and suffered heavy losses.

The harsh Afghan winter and impossible passage of weapons and soldiers on the snow-blocked mountain passes restricted military activity in the region. Until the summer of 1992 no significant military actions were taken around Kabul.

The failure of Hekmatyar's forces in Kabul contributed to the reinforcement of his rival Sheikh Masud whose status, as previously mentioned, was rising. Towards the end of 1991 he became a key figure not only in the military realm but also in the political realm in the context of the Mujahidin movements.

In interviews given at the end of the war[2] Sheikh Masud presented pragmatic positions in which he expressed his desire to establish an Islamic republic which would combine the principles of Islam with the need to modernize his country.

He argued that an administration representative of all the ethnic groups and political and religious streams in Afghanistan should be established, but he nevertheless did not hesitate to take forceful action against rival factions, especially Hekmatyar's, when they challenged or threatened the new regime.[3]

As previously mentioned, a number of other commanders who formed significant political and economic power blocs rose during the war years, among them:

- **Ismael Khan**[4] – born in 1942, was recruited into the Afghan army and attained the rank of major.
  In March 1979 there was an Islamic uprising in Herat against the Communist regime of Mohammed Taraki. Ismael Khan, who was the commander of the force stationed in Herat, came to the aid of the rebels and assisted them in rebuffing forces loyal to the government.
  The uprising lasted five days until backup arrived for the government forces. Ismael Khan eventually fled Herat to the mountains with 60 of his men and continued resistance activity against the Communist regime.
  Ismael Khan and his people joined the Mujahidin movement headed by Rabbani. His courage and leadership in the field enabled him to advance rapidly in the organization's ranks of command.
  In 1984 he was appointed commander of the Mujahidin forces in the Herat region and due to his successes on the battlefield was called "the lion of Herat."
  In 1992, after the fall of Najibullah's regime, he was made responsible for the southwestern provinces of Afghanistan. As such he worked to dismantle the militias in the region, reinstate order and security, repair damage caused by the war and return refugees to their homes.
  In July 1994 Ismael Khan convened commanders from rival Mujahidin factions in an attempt to bring about national reconciliation and end the civil war, but failed.
  In 1995 Ismael Khan's forces were attacked by the Taliban and General Dostum's Uzbeki forces. When Ismael Khan realized that he could not withstand them he chose to retreat from Herat to spare it the destruction and ruin of siege and battle.

- **Abdul Haq** – was born in 1958 of Pashtun descent. He was the head of the Hizb-i-Islam forces in Kabul. Abdul Haq was arrested, tortured and sentenced to death in 1977 under Mohammed Daoud. Subsequent to the 1978 coup, Haq was released, went underground and established a militia that took extremely daring action against the Soviets in the Kabul region.
  In April 1982 Abdul Haq visited Paris as part of a delegation of Afghan Mujahidin leaders.[5]

- **Jalaluddin Haqqani** – of Pashtun descent, a member of the Hazdarhan tribe. During 1980-1984 he was allied with Gailani's movement but since 1984 has been a member of Khalis Younis' Hizb-e-Islami.

The Mujahidin Regime of Rabbani

The first years of the Mujahidin regime in Afghanistan under President Rabbani were marked by a lack of stability, severe power struggles between rival Mujahidin factions and increasing involvement of outside elements in the Afghan turmoil.

In accordance with the Jalalabad agreements, President Rabbani received a mandate for 18 months to establish a transitional government with representation of all Mujahidin factions. At the end of the period, there were to have been general elections a president and a new government. The mandate expired on June 28, 1994, and despite the time that had passed, the rival sides in Afghanistan seemed neither willing nor able to implementation the agreements and hold elections.[1]

At the root of the continued conflicts in Afghan society were the following issues:

- Personal and partisan power struggles between Mujahidin factions (the most prominent Mujahidin fighting each other were Rabbani against Hekmatyar and Dostum head of the Uzbeki militia)
- Power struggles for control between ethnic and religious groups: Pashtuns, Tajikis, Uzbekis and the Shiite Hazaras
- Outside involvement that encouraged internal dissension and conflict in Afghanistan.

Four main political and military elements sparred for control of Afghanistan:

- The regime, headed by President Rabbani and Minister of Defense Sheikh Masud who represented the Tajiki minority and were dependent on a

relatively narrow coalition with other Mujahidin organizations mainly from the traditional factions
- The regime's main rival Hekmatyar, head of the Hizb-e-Islam movement which represented the Pashtun majority in the country and had the most radical Islamic orientation among the Mujahidin movements
- General Dostum at the head of the Uzbeki militia and who identified with the Uzbeki minority in Afghanistan
- A group of Shiite organizations representing the Hazara minority in Afghanistan and supported by Iran.

General Dostum's moves are striking examples of the political opportunism characteristic of the political system. Towards the end of the battles of the Mujahidin headed by Rabbani and Sheikh Masud against Najibullah's regime, General Dostum and his militia (the Islamic National Party) crossed over to the Mujahidin side. As a result of his help in conquering Kabul, he achieved control over parts of the city and the northern provinces of the country in which the Uzbeki minority lived. In battles that broke out in April 1992 between Rabbani's and Hekmatyar's forces, Dostum's followers fought on Rabbani's side and helped him to defend Kabul. At the start of 1993, in battles between Rabbani's and Hekmatyar's forces, Dostum took a neutral stance because of disagreements between himself and Rabbani over control of the northern provinces of the country.[2] In January 1994, the regime in Kabul thwarted an attempted coup initiated by Hekmatyar, Dostum and Babrak Karmal (the Communist ex-president). The attempted coup was accompanied by local battles in the capital, battles in which the government forces had the advantage.[3]

General Dostum, as the above examples attest, changed his orientation and support three times in a period of three years: from supporting the Communist regime in Kabul to supporting the Mujahidin then, in power struggles between Mujahidin factions, from support for Rabbani to neutrality, and finally to support of Hekmatyar.

The attempted coup of January 1994 is strong testimony to the opportunism characterizing the Afghan political system because it shows the willingness of ideologically polarized forces (Karmal the Communist and Hekmatyar, one of the most extreme Afghan Islamic fundamentalists) to cooperate *ad hoc* to achieve common short-term objectives. The Afghan political system was characterized by severe dissension, splitting and lack of stability, with Rabbani's regime facing constant threat from both old and new political rivals.

Replacement of the secular regime in Kabul by a Mujahidin regime did not bring about the end of the civil war but opened a new chapter of struggle for control between Mujahidin movements. In this struggle, as mentioned, the coalition headed by Rabbani had the advantage. However, the Islamic regime in Kabul under Rabbani failed to impose its authority over all the territories in the country. Parts remained in the hands of opposition Mujahidin movements led mainly by its rival Hekmatyar (head of the Hizb-e-Islami).

The lack of political stability and continued conflict with the opposition prevented the regime and the population from working toward rehabilitation of the infrastructure and economy that had been destroyed by years of war.

The struggle for control of Afghanistan after the fall of the Communist regime was no longer an ideological conflict or a battle for national liberation; it became a struggle for power and control between the leaders of the movements, nourished and motivated by ethnic and regional interests as well.

The endless clashes resulted in a state of anarchy in Afghanistan, with the central government controlling Kabul while, elsewhere in the country, commanders of military militias and heads of Mujahidin movements did as they pleased in the areas they held.

It was against this gloomy background that the Taliban movement emerged in the early 1990s – a movement that within a short space of time changed the political and military power balance in the country.

The Taliban Movement – Roots and Ideology

The Taliban movement grew out of the Islamic schools in Pakistan. The term *talibi* means pupil or student of Islam in both Arabic and Farsi (*taliban* in plural).

Unlike most of the Afghan Mujahidin movements which emerged in Afghanistan and Pakistan in the context of the struggle (Jihad) against the Communist regime in Kabul and its Soviet allies, the Taliban was established in the early 1990s after the Mujahidin movements already ruled Afghanistan.

The movement developed from a sense of frustration with the civil war between Mujahidin factions which continued after expulsion of the Communist regime, a frustration felt by significant portions of the Afghan population in both Afghanistan and the refugee camps in Pakistan.

Rabbani's government did not succeed in imposing its rule on most of Afghanistan. It remained ruptured, divided and under the control of various Mujahidin factions with local militia leaders doing as they pleased in the regions under their control.

The anarchistic reality prevented any practical possibility of rebuilding the ruin the country had suffered in 13 years of civil war and returning the millions of Afghan refugees who had fled to Pakistan and Iran.

The Taliban believed that Rabbani's government and most of the rival Mujahidin movements in Afghanistan did not properly practice the laws of Islam (in the spirit of Shariah) and were far from forming the Islamic state they had pledged to establish during the struggle against the Communists.

The Taliban movement therefore emerged as a social and religious movement that hoped to change the anarchic face of Afghanistan, turning it into a true Islamic state according to the interpretation and understanding of its founders.

The founders and members of the Taliban movement came from the ranks of the Islamic school in Pakistan, with the city of Binori near Karachi as the nucleus for movement members. From here came the leader of the movement, Mullah Mohammed Omar, and at least three members of the movement's governing council.

The Taliban led an ascetic lifestyle centered around religious studies that began each day with morning prayers at dawn and ended in the evening, with only short breaks for food and prayer during the day.

Studies lasted three years. During the first year the students learned the Koran by heart and afterwards focused on Islamic religious laws and precepts.

The Taliban called their schools "Sunni Deobandi" after the Deobandis[1] who had been part of the reform movements that emerged in the 18th century with the aim of purifying Islam of streams and movements that adopted interpretations and customs that deviated from the direct commandments of the Koran, Shariah and belief in Mohammed. (Examples of these beliefs were worship of later saints, prayers at the tombs of saints, etc.)

The Taliban adopted the strict Hanafi interpretation[2] as a mandatory philosophy and, like the Deobandis, embarked on a struggle to impose what they saw as "true Islam" in Afghanistan.

Taliban rivals claim that the Taliban movement did not emerge spontaneously and naturally as an Islamic reform movement, but was in fact established by the Pakistani intelligence services to further Pakistani interests in the Afghan arena (see elaboration below.[3]

The Taliban movement and Pakistan's governments have categorically denied this allegation, but there is no doubt that the Taliban enjoyed informal support from political elements and organizations in Pakistan.

The Taliban's most prominent ally in Pakistan is the Jamiat-e-Ulema-a-Islam (JUI),[4] a radical Islamic political movement represented in the Pakistani parliament and a member of the coalition that made up Benazir Bhutto's last government.

The movement operates an extensive religious school system, which serves as a source for some volunteers recruited into the Taliban ranks. In October 1997 the Pakistani movement held a major publicity campaign to unite all the Islamic movements and organizations in Pakistan in support of the Taliban movement.

Pakistan's former minister of internal affairs (in Benazir Bhutto's government), Naseerullah Babar, was considered the architect and driving force behind Pakistani support for the establishment of the Taliban and supports it politically to this day.[5]

Franz Schurmann[6] suggests that the roots of the Taliban movement were among the groups of Afghan students who were influenced in the 1970s by the social messages of Chinese Maoism. The rise of the dictatorial Communist regime in Afghanistan in 1978 brought about the development of these groups and their return to faith in Islam. They felt that the social message and mission of Maoism was commensurate with Islam, and that Mao's doctrine of guerilla war was also compatible with the military struggle, at first against the regime in Kabul and then against the post-Communist rulers.

Professor Musa Maarufi[7] argues that the Taliban phenomenon has been part of the social and cultural fabric of Afghanistan since the arrival of Islam but that for most of history they had occupied themselves with religious study and avoided political activity.

The Taliban movement initially established religious groups on the political and military fronts and led them to conquer ninety percent of the territory of the country and control these areas.

At any rate the Taliban is a revolutionary movement motivated by an Islamic world view and a social purpose aimed at establishing a pure and just Islamic society in Afghanistan, although its messages and aspirations are not limited to within the official borders of the country.

Mullah Mohammed Omar

Mullah Mohammed Omar is the spiritual and political leader of the Taliban movement. Biographical details about him are scarce and as a rule he avoids giving interviews to the media.

Mohammed Omar is the son of a family of Pashtun farmers from the Kandahar region. In the wake of the Soviet invasion of Afghanistan, which took place when he was sixteen, his family fled to Peshawar in Pakistan and joined the millions of Afghan refugees living in the refugee camps there.

Mohammed Omar was educated in a Madrasa (religious school), and there was recruited for the Jihad against the Soviets in Afghanistan. After a short training period at a Mujahidin training facility, Mohammed Omar became a Mujahidin fighter in Younis Khalis' movement (the Islamic party). He served as a regular fighter and demonstrated leadership and courage which resulted in his appointment as commander of a regiment-sized force after two years. During the war he was injured and lost an eye.[8]

Following his father's death in a refugee camp in Pakistan, Mohammed Omar returned his family to the area of Kandahar.

When the Jihad against the Soviets was over, despite his youth, Mohammed

Omar established his own Madrasa and thanks to his charisma soon attracted a growing group of followers and supporters. In light of the anarchy that prevailed in Afghanistan after the Mujahidin's victory, Mohammed Omar decided to establish the Taliban movement – his goal was to change the reality in his country and set up an Islamic state in accordance with his ideology. In 1996 Mohammed Omar was crowned Emir of the Believers by a convention of religious Muslim sages in Kandahar – a religious title that accords him a great deal of status in the entire community of Muslim believers.

Mullah Mohammed Omar settled in Kandahar, a city of religious importance in Afghanistan because of the cloak of the prophet Mohammed, which tradition holds is preserved in the local mosque. From there he managed the Taliban regime and hardly visited the capital Kabul.

According to unverified information, one of Mohammed Omar's sisters is married to Bin Laden, while Mohammed Omar himself married Bin Laden's oldest daughter in 1998.

Mullah Mohammed Omar heads the collective leadership of the Taliban movement. The country was governed by three councils (see chart in Appendix C): (1) the central (high) council which was located in Kandahar and responsible for main decision making, and under it two other councils: (2) the military council and (3) the Kabul council – which acted as a government and whose members included most of the ministers and some of the military leaders.

Taliban Military Forces

Information about the structure of the Taliban military system is relatively scarce, although according to the little that is known it can be described as follows (see chart in Appendix C):

The supreme commander of the Taliban forces was the leader of the movement Mullah Mohammed Omar, who was also the head of the central (high) council. The military council, headed by the chief of staff and the chiefs of the land and air forces was subordinate to him. The fighting forces were divided into units that were analogous to divisions: four infantry divisions and an artillery division, which was usually stationed in Kabul. There seemed to be a kind of command force that can control the operative control of the divisions on the front.

The military council was responsible for strategic planning and force and equipment building, but every significant decision required the approval of the central council and Mullah Mohammed Omar. The chief of staff and chiefs of land and air forces were responsible for the operational and administrative management of the forces.

The Taliban forces had no clear definitions of ranks. Commanders were selected and appointed on merit and their sources of support (tribes, organizations, etc.).

Another extraordinary phenomenon was that ministers and members of the central council and Kabul council could also be military commanders. For example Mullah Mohammed Abas, the Minister of Health, was deputy commander of Taliban forces in the battles near Mazar-e-Sharif in 1997. After that he was charged with building another force in Herat in preparation for a new attack in Mazar-e-Sharif, after which he returned to his position as Minister of Health. Likewise, Mullah Ahsanullah, the chairman of the Central Taliban Bank, commanded a thousand soldiers in battles near Mazar-e-Sharif, in which he was subsequently killed. Actually, most of the members of the central council and the Kabul council, excluding the disabled ones among them, simultaneously held military command positions.

This system created a direct and close connection between the government and administration and the fighting forces, although the extended absence of the members of the council who also served as ministers in the Taliban government was severely detrimental to the efficiency of the country's administrative system. According to this system Mullah Mohammed Omar could send one or another minister who has gained too much power, to the front at any time, or bring him back. The Taliban's governmental and military system was therefore strong, flexible and unstable all at the same time, with no definite patterns and rules of action.

This system of command and management, which is based on a nucleus of leaders and commanders who created and maintained a common language based on deep understanding of common ideas and goals, struggled to synchronize the minor bureaucratic (technocratic) system. The latter had remained in place from previous regimes and therefore only knew how to operate according to clear and graduated patterns of action. This system, of course, also prevented the integration of members of ethnic minorities – Tajikis, Uzbekis and Hazaras – within the governmental system and the ranks of the Taliban military.

Military personnel was derived from three sources:

1. The nucleus of a professional military (permanent force) based in part on professional soldiers who served during the Communist regime, in armored, artillery, air forces and others.

2. Recruits who were drafted by a conscription order issued by the Taliban in the areas they controlled.
3. Volunteers from religious schools in Pakistan (who made up 30% of the Taliban army).

Recruits and volunteers from Pakistan usually served for relatively short periods, then returned home and were replaced by new blood.

The Taliban forces, due to these systems of recruitment, usually did not number more than thirty thousands soldiers, but in preparation for important battles recruitment was increased and discharges delayed so that the extent of the forces could reach fifty thousand soldiers.

The Taliban's personnel management system matched the traditional Pashtun tribal approach, where volunteers and recruits were absorbed in a short period of time in preparation for war and at the end of the war returned to their daily routines (this system was called Lashkar).

With respect to equipment, the Taliban movement received assistance at the outset from weapons and ammunition supplied by Pakistan, but after the Taliban seized most of the territory of Afghanistan they gained access to the majority of the state's weapons and munitions reserves, enough to meet most of their needs on the battlefield.

The Taliban and the Road to Power

The Taliban movement began its political and military activity in the city of Kandahar in southern Afghanistan.

There are a number of reasons why Kandahar was selected as the starting point for building up the movement's power and strength:

First, Kandahar is the birthplace of Mullah Omar, founder and leader of the movement. Second, Kandahar is located in a region dominated by Pashtuns, from which the movement emerged. Third, Kandahar is a city with religious significance for Muslims (since 1751).

The movement took control of Kandahar via political moves that resulted in some of the local militia commanders joining the movement, and quick military strikes that resulted in the surrender of militia commanders who resisted.

From the beginning, the movement learned to employ unusual means, including an extensive publicity campaign warning that harm to the Taliban – who were described as religious figures – was tantamount to harm to Islam.[1]

The movement also learned to play the divisions and rivalries between factions in the various Mujahidin movements and military militias in order to recruit some of them to its ranks and create preferential power relations that would make it relatively easy to quash the remaining pockets of resistance. Kandahar became, therefore, the Taliban's main area of power and influence. From there, the movement spread to other parts of the country.[2]

In a short period of time, the Taliban succeeded in enforcing Islamic law in Kandahar and reinstating order and security for a population that had suffered from a lack of law and order for almost twenty years. The Taliban's success in Kandahar led to many Pashtuns in the south joining its ranks because they saw in the Taliban hope for returning to a normal way of life and ending the country's civil war and anarchy.

In the first months after its establishment, the Taliban's main efforts focused on securing influence and control over the Pashtun population.

For this reason the Taliban first undertook a struggle against Hekmatyar's movement which, until the appearance of the Taliban, had been the major political and military player among the Pashtun population.

In late 1994 Hekmatyar was embroiled in fierce battles against Rabbani's regime and was also at odds with most of the leaders and commanders of the other Mujahidin movements.

The Taliban took advantage of Hekmatyar's weakness and occupation with the struggle against Rabbani's government. Within a few months (October 1994-February 1995), the Taliban conquered most of Hekmatyar's strongholds in the south of the country and around Kabul. (See table of milestones on the Taliban's road to power.)

During these months Rabbani's government encouraged the Taliban's activities and saw it as an ally in the confrontation with Hekmatyar and the Shiite Hizb-e-Wahadat. In battles around Kabul in February 1995 the forces of Rabbani's government took advantage of the military pressure the Taliban was putting on Hekmatyar from the south and conquered most of his strongholds around Kabul. But the alliance between the Rabbani government and the Taliban was short-lived. As early as March 1995 Masud and Rabbani understood, perhaps too late, that they themselves had created an incalculable threat against their rule by helping the Taliban gain victory and advance toward Kabul.

On March 9, 1995, after Hekmatyar's forces around Kabul had been defeated, the Taliban reached an agreement with Hizb-e-Wahadat which resulted in the retreat of the Shiites and transfer of their positions around Kabul to the Taliban.

At this stage it was clear to the Rabbani government that the Taliban was threatening Kabul directly. Therefore on March 10 their forces launched an extensive attack which forced the Taliban to retreat from the Kabul area.

The government forces' attack on the Taliban led to the latter's first defeat on the battlefield since the beginning of its campaign in October 1994, and was a turning point in the Afghan civil war. From March 1995 on, most of the struggle took place between the Taliban and the Rabbani government, with other militias becoming pawns of these two in the struggle for control of Afghanistan.

In the ensuing months (March-September 1995) the Taliban continued to fight government forces, especially around Kabul, while the government was also facing forces of the Shiite Hizb-e-Wahadat, Dostum's Uzbeki militias and Hekmatyar on other fronts, mainly in the north and west of Afghanistan.

A significant development took place on September 5, 1995, when the Taliban conquered the important provincial city of Herat from Ismail Khan, an ally of the Rabbani government.

Conquest of this city, mainly inhabited by Tajikis and Shiites, heightened the ethnic aspect of the struggle between the Pashtun Taliban and the Shiite and Tajiki minorities in Afghanistan.

On September 13 the Rabbani government initiated mass demonstrations outside Pakistan's embassy in Kabul and publicly blamed Pakistan for involvement in Afghanistan's internal affairs via its protege, the Taliban.

A formal rift was thus created between the Rabbani government and the Pakistani government which, despite its official denial of connections with the Taliban, continued to support the movement through financial and military aid.

The success of the Taliban movement led to the end of Pakistan's support for Hekmatyar's movement. His political and military isolation caused him to try to temporarily improve his relations with the Rabbani government and form a coalition with the Hizb-e-Wahadat and Dostum the Uzbeki.

In October 1995, encouraged by their victory in Herat, the Taliban decided for the second time to conquer Kabul. They were however forced to make do with conquering a number of strategic areas around the city. Their attempts to penetrate the suburbs of Kabul were rebuffed by the Rabbani government forces.

In the months that followed, static fighting around Kabul and in other parts of the country continued with no significant progress made by the Taliban.

During this time the movement cemented its control in the regions it had captured, with Kandahar serving as the movement's center of control and influence.

In April 1996, 1000 senior religious leaders from throughout Afghanistan met and elected the leader of the Taliban, Mullah Omar, the Emir of the Believers, and divested Rabbani and his government of their religious authority.

The declaration of Mohammed Omar as Emir of the Believers was an important milestone in consolidation of the Taliban movement and its leader's status as a political religious entity supported by the Sunni religious establishment, which is very influential in Afghan society.

The Taliban continued to secure its control in regions that covered close to two-thirds of the territory of Afghanistan while the Rabbani government's dominance was in practice limited to Kabul and part of the northern provinces inhabited by Tajikis.

The Taliban simultaneously continued to build their military strength in preparation for a decisive attack on the forces of the Rabbani government which began in September 1996.

On September 11, 1996, the Taliban launched an extensive battle in eastern Afghanistan, conquering two provinces that the government had held as well as the important city of Jalalabad, thus opening an important logistical artery along the Pakistani border.

After the conquest of Jalalabad, the thrust of the Taliban's offensive was transferred to Kabul and Taliban forces began to effect a closure and siege of the city.

On the night of September 26, 1996, the Rabbani government and the forces it commanded (mainly Sheikh Masud, the Tajiki minister of defense's forces) left Kabul and retreated northwards to Tajiki populated areas that were controlled by forces loyal to Sheikh Masud. On September 27, 1996, the Taliban forces entered Kabul with almost no resistance, took control of the city and seized rule of Afghanistan.

The Rabbani government claimed that this was a temporary tactical retreat to prevent unnecessary civilian casualties in Kabul and that it remained the legal government of Afghanistan. In practice, however, the government had lost all its power and command of the country. The Taliban quickly established a governing council which reigned over most of the Afghan territory and population.

The fall of Kabul into the hands of the Taliban did not bring about the end of the civil war. A short time after retreating from Kabul, the Tajikis Rabbani and Masud established a coalition with General Dostum the Uzbeki and the Shiite Hizb-e-Wahadat and continued the struggle against the Taliban.[3]

The coalition had the support of Iran, Russia and the Muslim republics on the Afghan border (Turkmenistan, Uzbekistan, Tajikistan), which viewed the Taliban victory as a threat to their interests and the ethnic groups affiliated with them.

The fall of the Rabbani government and the Taliban takeover of Kabul gave the civil war in Afghanistan an overt ethnic and religious flavor, with the Taliban representing the Sunni Pashtun majority against the ethnic Sunni minorities of Tajikis and Uzbekis and the Shiite Hizb-e-Wahadat.

In late 1996 the Taliban tried to take political steps intended to crumble the opposition and draw the Uzbeki General Dostum – whose opportunistic approach was apparent throughout the civil war – temporarily to their side. When these attempts failed, the Taliban launched a renewed military attack to conquer the rest of the country from the hands of the opposition.[4]

In January 1997 the Taliban conquered the important airport in Bagram north of Kabul, but their attempts to progress further north into the Panjshir valley, the power center of the Tajiki Sheikh Masud, failed. In May 1997 the Taliban launched an attack to conquer the provincial city of Mazar-e-Sharif, the main stronghold of Uzbeki and Shiite forces in the north.[5]

The Taliban took advantage of internal power struggles in the Uzbeki camp between General Dostum and his deputy General Malik, who along with his forces defected to the Taliban side, forcing General Dostum to flee by air to Turkey. Through this unholy alliance the Taliban conquered Mazar-e-Sharif.[6]

But the alliance was short-lived. When General Malik discovered that the Taliban intended to divest the militias in the city of their arms, he launched a surprise attack on the Taliban, killing thousands and taking many captive.[7]

Malik's betrayal cost the Taliban one of their most severe defeats (the bodies of some 3000 Taliban warriors were found in the Mazar-e-Sharif area and hundreds of commanders and soldiers were taken captive by the Uzbekis) and the thwarting of a move which might have isolated Rabbani and Masud in the struggle against the Taliban.[8]

After the failure at Mazar-e-Sharif, fighting between the Taliban and the opposition continued on the northern fronts, but with neither side able to achieve a decisive outcome.

In October 1997 the Taliban tried a second time to conquer Mazar-e-Sharif but Uzbeki forces under General Malik managed to hold off the attack. This time it was General Dostum who grabbed the opportunity. While General Malik was busy rebuffing the Taliban, he returned to Afghanistan. Within a day, the forces loyal to him ousted General Malik and reinstated his control over most of the Uzbeki areas in the country. (The political system of the Uzbeki minority will be elaborated upon below.)

Since October 1997 the Taliban and opposition forces have been fighting on various fronts in the north of the country with no military decision in sight, especially because of massive military aid that Iran provided to Shiite and Uzbeki forces. Nevertheless, Mazar e Sharif was finally conquered by the Taliban in August 1998.

Opposition elements also waged terror against the Taliban regime. On August 25, 1999, there was an attempted assassination of leader Mullah Mohammed Omar, when his vehicle arrived at Kandahar (the Taliban's center of power) after a visit to Herat. An explosive device exploded near his car, injuring him lightly and killing six of his bodyguards.[9]

At the same time, efforts were made by various parties to reach an agreement that would bring about the end of the civil war in Afghanistan, with no success. (The diplomatic efforts to reach a peace settlement will be elaborated on below.)[10]

Milestones on the Taliban's Road to Power

August 1994 –	Mohammed Omar Aqond, the Mullah of Kandahar, establishes the Taliban movement.
October 13, 1994 –	First military confrontation between the Taliban and Hekmatyar's forces.
November 5, 1994 –	Taliban forces conquer the city of Kandahar from Hekmatyar's forces.
November 29, 1994 –	The Rabbani government declares its support for the Taliban initiative to instill order on the roads, open them and remove the various militia checkpoints.
January 25, 1995 –	Rabbani government forces and Taliban forces cooperate in defending the city of Ghanzi south of Kabul against an attack by Hekmatyar's forces.
February 4-10, 1995 –	Taliban forces conquer most of the Waradak province in eastern Afghanistan from Hekmatyar's forces and control six of the thirty Afghan provinces.
February 11, 1995 –	Under pressure from the Taliban, Hekmatyar is forced to abandon his base in Charasyab near Kabul. Rabbani government forces take advantage of his weakness and conquer most of his positions around the capital of Kabul. As a result, Hekmatyar's allies, the Shiite Hizb-e-Wahadat forces, are isolated on the battlefront around Kabul.

March 9, 1995 –	The Hizb-e-Wahadat reaches an agreement with the Taliban, retreats from its positions on the Kabul front in Karteseh and hands them over to the Taliban.
March 11-12, 1995 –	The Rabbani government comprehends the threat from the Taliban for the first time, and launches a surprise attack on the Taliban and the Hizb-e-Wahadat, forcing them to retreat from Kabul. This is the Taliban's first defeat. After retreat they continue fighting against the Rabbani government's forces around the city.
March-December 1995 –	Period when most of the fighting around Kabul between the Taliban and Rabbani government takes place. At the same time the government forces have to deal with the Hizb-e-Wahadat, Hekmatyar and General Dostum's militia in the north.
September 5, 1995 –	The Taliban conquer Herat from Ismael Khan, an ally of Rabbani. Conquest of the city, which is populated mainly by Dari speaking Shiites, heightens the ethnic conflict between the Pashtun Taliban and the Shiites and Tajikis.
September 13, 1995 –	The Rabbani government initiates mass demonstrations outside the Pakistani embassy in Kabul, publicly blames Pakistan for involvement in Afghanistan's internal affairs by means of the Taliban movement. The Pakistani government and the Taliban deny the allegations.
October 1995 –	The Taliban reach the outskirts of Kabul for the second time, conquering Charasyab, Rishkor and the Khairabad hills. The siege around Kabul grows tighter.
April 1996 –	One thousand Muslim religious leaders elect Mullah Mohammed Omar as the Emir of the Believers and discharge Rabbani and his government as the Islamic leaders of the Afghan nation.
June 1996 –	Taliban forces conquer Chaghcharam, capital of the Ghor province, and launch a heavy missile attack on Kabul (54 dead and 118 wounded). Hekmatyar becomes Rabbani's prime minister.

September 11, 1996 –	The Taliban launch a large attack in eastern Afghanistan, conquering Jalalabad and two other provinces.
September 27, 1996 –	The Taliban conquer Kabul with almost no resistance and government forces retreat north to Tajiki controlled regions.
September-October, 1996 –	The Taliban establish their rule in Kabul and enforce an extremist Islamic regime.
January 1997 –	The Taliban conquer the airport in Bagram, north of Kabul.
April 1997 –	The Taliban announce the exposure and thwarting of an attempted rebellion in the eastern provinces of Afghanistan.
May 1997 –	The Taliban conquer Mazar-e-Sharif, the main stronghold of Shiite Uzbeki opposition in the north, but are expelled from it a short time later.
October 1997 –	The Taliban make a second attempt to conquer Mazar-e-Sharif and fail.
August 1998 –	The Taliban conquer Mazar-e-Sharif.

The Taliban Regime – Main Characteristics

Mullah Mohammed Omar, elected Emir of the Believers in April 1996, served as head of the Taliban movement and of the Afghan state. In October 1997 the Taliban changed the name of the country from the "Islamic Republic of Afghanistan" to the "Islamic Emirate of Afghanistan," a change which conveys the religious-legal significance the Taliban wish to impart to their rule.

The country is led by the Emir and a six-member ruling council. Some council members are also ministers in the government. The country is run according of the laws of Shariah and Afghan citizens are required to lead orthodox Islamic lifestyles.

Islamic law is enforced by deterrents, punishment and terror, which elicit harsh criticism from international human rights organizations and even from neighboring Iran which, until the Taliban came to power, was perceived as the symbol of Islamic fundamentalism.[1]

The Taliban's cruel attitude toward political and military adversaries and anyone who deviates from the commandments of Islam (as the Taliban interpret them) is one of the main instruments of their victory. The element of deterrence worked on many commanders and soldiers in rival militias and movements who chose to defect to the Taliban rather than oppose them and risk the punishments awaiting them should they be captured in battle.

Well-documented testimony of the Taliban's merciless approach is their treatment of the former president of Afghanistan, Najibullah, and his brother. After the conquest of Kabul, members of the movement stormed the UN building where Najibullah and his brother were hiding, beat them mercilessly and then hanged them from electricity poles in the central square of Kabul. A short time afterward two of Najibullah's bodyguards were also hanged.[2]

The Taliban strictly enforced Islamic law in all areas under their control but received international attention mainly after they took over Kabul and put in place a strict Islamic lifestyle in a city that until then had enjoyed more exposure to Western lifestyles and had a higher percentage of foreign nationals than other regions. As soon as the city was conquered, the Taliban announced that women were forbidden to work outside the home and girls were not permitted to attend school. The prohibition on women working was an extremely harsh blow to the income of many families in Kabul, especially those of 25,000 war widows who were the sole breadwinners in their families.[3]

Outside their homes, women are required to wear a "*burka*" which covers them from head to foot, and be accompanied by a male relative.

Women who deviate from these directives are punished by special bands of Taliban who oversee the enforcement of Islamic law.[4]

Infractions such as an unmarried woman and man being found together, or adultery, are brought before special courts located throughout the cities and are likely to end in a sentence of death by stoning. Men in Afghanistan are required to keep the commandment of praying in mosques, wear traditional dress, grow a beard and have their hair cut according to religious guidelines.

In November 1997, roadblocks were set up throughout Kabul. Pedestrians and passengers are taken from their vehicles to have their haircuts inspected. Should they be found inappropriate (long hair that covers part of the forehead), they are shaved on the spot by Taliban barbers.

A Taliban member explained to a Western media team that long hair on a Muslim man's head enables Satan to nest in it.[5]

The Taliban also implemented criminal law in the spirit of Shariah. Special courts discuss the fate of criminals in flash trials without allowing the defendants representation by lawyers or appeal procedures. Verdicts are handed down immediately, according to Islamic Shariah law, and include the amputation of limbs of thieves, or executions by firing squad or occasionally by a member of the victim's family in cases of murder or bodily harm.

The strict enforcement of Islamic law has brought about a drastic drop in the crime rate in a country that for almost twenty years had known no law and order. Therefore, although the Taliban's policies received severe criticism from outside the country, it enjoyed significant support from many Afghan citizens who enjoyed the quiet and relative security.[6]

Nevertheless, the Taliban movement wields a reign of personal and collective terror towards ethnic minorities suspected of disloyalty to the Taliban, groups considered ex-Communists and political rivals.[7]

A result of this policy is that thousands of Afghan citizens are in prison. In many areas, members of ethnic minorities fled from the Taliban to areas controlled by their own people. A new movement of mainly Tajiki and Shiite refugees are fleeing Kabul to the Tajiki north and to areas in western Afghanistan controlled by Shiites. The Taliban called on Afghan citizens in refugee camps in Pakistan to return to Afghanistan but the response has been relatively limited and mostly include members of Pashtun groups who identify with the Taliban.

The Taliban succeeded in establishing a regime of law and order in the spirit of Islam in most areas under their control, but they were facing significant difficulties in their efforts to provide services and meet the basic needs of the population.

After twenty years of war the economic infrastructure was in ruin and the country's coffers empty. The Taliban government is therefore forced to accept aid from international organizations and contributions from various countries to provide food and basic medical services for the population.

The policy of brutal enforcement of Islamic law and the Taliban's inherent hostility to the West create many points of conflict which lessen the willingness of Western countries and international aid organizations to aid Afghanistan.

Moreover, protracted fighting against the opposition has forced the Taliban to invest their limited resources in the war in the north, at the expense of rehabilitating the country.

During the civil war, opium cultivation and the drug trade was the primary source of income for the Mujahidin factions in Afghanistan. The Taliban accused Rabbani's government of corruption and encouraging the drug trade. In spite of the Taliban declarations, the export of drugs from the opium-growing regions in Afghanistan under Taliban control continued (export of heroin from Afghanistan is estimated at millions of dollars per year).[8]

Sources amongst the opposition claim that senior Taliban officials deal directly in the cultivation and trade of drugs and that opium production in Afghanistan in 1999 in Taliban-controlled provinces reached 400 tons, most of which was sent through Turkmenistan and Iran to Europe and the USA.[9]

The Anti-Taliban Coalition (The Northern Alliance)

The Taliban conquest of Kabul and the fall of Rabbani's government led to a significant change in Afghanistan's political and military balance of power. Former rivals and adversaries formed a new coalition with the main common denominator being fear of the Taliban gaining control of the rest of the areas still in their hands.

The coalition, called the "United Islamic Front" or the "Northern Allicance" includes the following organizations:[1]

- **The Rabbani government** (which claims that it is the legal and recognized government of Afghanistan) and forces under its control, mainly the Tajiki militia commanded by Sheikh Ahmed Masud
- **General Dostum's Uzbeki militia**
- **The Hizb-e-Wahadat** – an umbrella organization of seven Shiite movements
- **Hekmatyar and the remnants of his forces.**

Coordination between the various components of the coalition is weak. In practice, each movement fights to defend its own areas. Topographical conditions make coordination and mutual assistance difficult, especially between the Tajiki forces in the northeast and the Uzbeki and Shiite forces in the northwest.

There was closer cooperation in the political realm, with each component of the coalition still formally represented in Rabbani's government and coordination taking place regarding contacts with various mediators in the negotiations towards a peace settlement with the Taliban.

The most visible characteristic of the Afghan internal front was the creation of clear lines of conflict between the different ethnic groups. The Taliban, representing the Pashtun majority, were trying to seize complete control of the country by attempting to defeat the main ethnic minorities: the Tajikis, the Uzbekis and the Shiites. The militias of the ethnic minorities were struggling to survive and maintain their autonomous political and military status in the presence of a very significant threat to their existence and status as political forces.

Until October 2001, it was clear to the coalition members that they would not be able to overcome the Taliban. Therefore, as a diplomatic solution, they advocated the establishment of a national unity government that will would their political and military status and a large degree of cultural and religious autonomy.[2]

The Taliban, on the other hand, were interested in a resolution that would give them total hegemony over the country, with the ethnic minorities receiving representation after their militias are dismantled, but with the absolute dominance of the Taliban being maintained.

The Taliban realized that if the ethnic minorities retain their military power under the terms of a settlement, their rule would be vulnerable at all times to threats from one or another coalition that could rise up against the Taliban.

Components of the anti-Taliban coalition represent not only the interests of the ethnic minorities living in Afghanistan, but also the interests of neighboring countries. Tajikistan and Uzbekistan see Rabbani, Masud and Dostum as a security buffer against the radical Islamic threat posed by the Taliban which openly declares its contempt for borders and aspiration to disseminate Islam.[3]

Even Iran sees the Shiite minorities in the west and north of Afghanistan as part of the apparatus for blocking the influence of the Taliban who are hostile to Shiism and Iran.

These countries are therefore interested in preventing the victory of the Taliban and in reaching settlement that would preserve the status of their proteges who would continue to provide a buffer between the Taliban and themselves.

The Taliban were aware of the weakness of the coalition, the conflicts of interest between its components and the personal and partisan rivalries within each, and did their best to force its collapse knowing that it would be easier to handle each component separately.

During 2000, elements close to the Taliban claimed that there had been a division in the ranks of Sheikh Masud as a result of his growing closeness with Russia. Groups with extremist Islamic orientation accused Masud of cooperating with the Russian (ex)enemy for personal reasons.[4]

At the same time the Taliban were putting pressure on patrons, especially

Iran, to reduce the military aid they supply to the militias on the grounds that this is involvement in the internal affairs of Afghanistan. They also accused Iran of attempts to prevent attainment of a peace settlement and the end of the civil war.[5]

In May 1997 the Taliban publicly accused Iran of subversive activity against its government, espionage and assisting the opposition. It closed the Iranian embassy in Kabul and deported the diplomatic staff.[6]

The Iranians, of course, denied the Taliban's allegations but there is overwhelming evidence that the coalition's successful defense of Mazar-e-Sharif in 1997 was based to a large degree on huge arms shipments from Iran.

According to various testimonies, the Mashad airport in Iran is a logistics base for flying supplies and equipment to the Uzbeki militia and the Hizb-e-Wahadat forces in the north and west of Afghanistan.[7]

Between May and June 1997 the tension between the Taliban and Iran was exacerbated by accusations of the kidnapping and murder of Iranian diplomats. The tension even led to the massing of Iranian forces on the common border and execution of maneuvers meant to signal to the Taliban that Iran would not condone the anti-Iranian policy of the Taliban government.

In August 1998, after heavy battles, the Taliban conquered the city of Mazar-e-Sharif and claimed to have captured thirty Iranians in the city who were providing equipment and arms to the opposition. They denied once again that Iranian diplomats had been kidnapped or murdered by their forces.[8]

Since 1999 the tension between the two countries has abated somewhat, but Taliban forces continue to fight against the Hizb-e-Wahadat and its allies, and Iranian support of the latter continues.[9]

On September 9, 2001, the anti-Taliban coalition suffered a serious blow when Sheikh Ahmed Masud was assassinated at his command post in the Panjshir valley. Two suicide bombers disguised as journalists, apparently sent by the Taliban and Bin Laden, met with Masud ostensibly to interview him for a newspaper and blew themselves up in his presence, killing him.

There are scholars who believe that there is a connection between Sheikh Ahmed Masud's assassination and the chain of attacks launched by Bin Laden two days later against American targets. According to this theory, Masud's death was meant to weaken the opposition at the critical stage when American response to the attacks launched on the heart of the USA was anticipated.

The Coalition Against the Taliban

The Political Umbrella
Government headed by Burhanuddin Rabbani*

Political Movements

The Islamic Movement of Afghanistan - Jamaat-e-Islami el-Afghani	The Uzbeki Movement	The Islamic Party Hizb-e-Islami	Hizb-e-Wahadat
Represents the Tajiki minority	Represents the Uzbeki minority	Based on Pashtun members	Represents the Shiite minority
Head: Rabbani	Head: General Dostum	Head: Hekmatyar	Head: Karim Khalili

The Militias

Ahmed Masud's militia	General Dostum's militia	Hekmatyar's militia	The militias of the movements united in the Hizb-e-Wahadat
Supporting countries: Russia Tajikistan Uzbekistan Iran	Supporting countries: Russia Uzbekistan Iran		Supporting country: Iran

* **Most Mujahidin factions are still formally represented by the Rabbani government.**

Internal Power Struggles among the Uzbekis

During 1979 an intense power struggle developed in the Uzbeki political and military movement between General Dostum, head of the movement and its military commander, and his deputy General Malik Pahlawan.

Competition between the two began in the early 1980s when they served in the same unit in the Afghan army (which at the time was Communist-oriented). Malik is a member of a rich Uzbeki family that controls substantial holdings of land in the Faryab area while Dostum is the son of a peasant family from the Jowzyan region. Despite Malik's higher status, Dostum progressed faster in his military service and was appointed commander of a division (consisting mainly of Uzbekis) that was stationed in the Kabul area.[1]

In 1992, when Mujahidin forces closed in on Kabul, Dostum and his forces defected to the Mujahidin side and helped overthrow Najibullah's regime. In return for his support, Dostum became a partner in Rabbani's coalition and, in effective, the ruler of the northern Uzbeki-inhabited provinces.

Dostum was assisted in his attempts to institute Uzbeki autonomy in northern Afghanistan by Malik's influential brother Rassul, who was governor of one of the northern provinces. Close cooperation developed between Dostum and Malik, who served as a foreign minister of sorts and coordinated the administrative work in the region.

Over the years, however, the rivalry between Dostum and Malik's family escalated. Dostum's family and followers were appointed to senior positions in Uzbeki centers of power and Malik and his family were gradually edged out of influential positions.

In June 1996 Rassul was murdered. Suspicion fell on Dostum, who around that time had had growing disputes with the family of Rassul and Malik.

In August 1996 fierce differences of opinion broke out between Malik and Dostum over the policy regarding the Taliban.[2] Malik tried to convince Dostum to pledge allegiance to the Taliban who were about to conquer Kabul. However, Dostum – who was under Russian and Iranian pressure – refused. He chose to back Rabbani's government and helped establish the anti-Taliban coalition.[3]

In February 1997 Dostum uncovered a plot to shoot down his helicopter with a Stinger missile. Dostum suspected that Malik was involved in this plot and began to monitor his deputy's every step.

In May 1997 General Malik launched a frontal conflict with Dostum. By means of soldiers loyal to him, he first took control of the capital of the province where his family lived (Mainama, capital of Faryab), then arrested tens of commanders with allegiance to Dostum and disarmed thousands of soldiers. At the same time he declared Dostum an anti-Islamic agent and initiated contact to form an alliance with the Taliban. Clashes between Dostum's and Malik's men quickly spread to all the Uzbeki provinces, while a broad Taliban attack on the Uzbeki provinces was simultaneously launched.

The attack was coordinated in advance with General Malik whose forces cooperated with the Taliban and forced Dostum's followers to flee to the mountainous regions of the north. Dostum himself barely escaped to Turkey.

The alliance between Malik and the Taliban paved the way for their conquest of the main provincial city that remained in the hands of the opposition, Mazar-e-Sharif, and its airport, an important hub for transfer of supplies to the opposition in the north.[4]

The alliance however was short-lived. Approximately a day after the Taliban entered Mazar-e-Sharif and Dostum fled Afghanistan, Malik changed his position. Together with the Shiite forces of the Hizb-e-Wahadat, he launched a surprise attack on the Taliban forces, causing them heavy losses, taking hundreds of prisoners and forcing the rest to flee Mazar-e-Sharif.[5]

The alliance between the Uzbeki militias, the Shiite forces and Sheik Masud's forces was renewed, this time with the Uzbeki forces under General Malik's command. From May to September 1997 stubborn fighting around Mazar-e-Sharif continued, with Taliban forces attempting to return and conquer the city. During this period Dostum continued, from his location at the time, to prepare the ground for his return to the fray.

In early October 1997 the Taliban launched a concentrated attack in an attempt to reconquer Mazar-e-Sharif. The attempt did not succeed however and the coalition forces retained their hold of most of the city's key positions.

On October 23, 1997, a short time after the fighting waned around Mazar-e-

, forces loyal to Dostum launched a surprise attack on General Malik's forces.[6]

Malik's followers put up only a minimal fight and within a few hours Malik was forced to escape by helicopter to Mashhad in Iran while his two brothers, Nuradin and Mohammed Pahlawan, fled to Faryab province, the main stronghold of the Malik family.[7]

Dostum's move appears to have been supported by the Shiite Hizb-e-Wahadat forces, which suspected General Malik of involvement in the murder of one of their leaders.

In November 1997 mass graves containing 5000 bodies were found in the region that had been under Malik's control. Dostum accused Malik of massacre and demanded that Iran extradite him so he could stand trial for his crimes. So far, this demand has not been met by Iranian authorities.[8] It seems that Dostum's victory in the internal struggles of the Uzbeki community is not the final word in this chapter.

Involvement of Outside Agents in the Civil War in Afghanistan

The internal conflict in Afghanistan is fostered to a large extent by the involvement of its neighbors and distant countries that derive political and military benefits from the ongoing strife.

Some neighboring countries are traditional patrons of Afghan ethnic groups and Mujahidin movements. By supporting these elements, they prevent attainment of a resolution or compromise in the Afghan internal dispute.

The following are neighboring countries that support the conflict (the attitudes of Pakistan and Iran towards the Taliban are elaborated below):

- **Pakistan** – supported Hekmatyar's movement in the past and later supports the Taliban.
- **Iran** – supports the coalition of Shiite movements in Afghanistan.
- **Muslim republics of the CIS** – Uzbekistan, Tajikistan and Turkmenistan support the coalition of General Dostum's Uzbeki militias and Rabbani and Masud's Tajiki forces which are fighting the Taliban regime and control the northern provinces of Afghanistan. These republics see the coalition forces as a security buffer protecting them against infiltration of radical Islamic influences from the Taliban.

A joint policy relating to the Taliban was formulated at a summit of the heads of the CIS republics in Alma Ata, capital of Kazakhstan. The policy constitutes mainly a demand that the Taliban ensure that internal Afghan struggles do not spill over into neighboring countries. In exchange, the CIS promises to abstain from involvement in Afghan internal affairs.

Together with fear and tension between the sides, there is coordination of economic interests, mainly regarding the laying of a natural gas and oil pipeline from Turkmenistan through Afghanistan to Pakistan. Turkmenistan is also involved in infrastructure projects such as road paving in Afghanistan in cooperation with Pakistan.[1]

More distant countries involved in the Afghan turmoil, each for its own reasons, include the following:

- **Russia** – saw the past Mujahidin and the current Taliban regimes as tangible threats to the Muslim republics in the CIS and to Russian interests in the region. Russian fears were reinforced when evidence emerged of involvement of Afghan fighters not only in fighting between peripheral pro-Russian regimes and Islamic movements (as in Uzbekistan and Tajikistan) but also in the war in Chechniya.[2]

Despite reassurances and warnings from Taliban leaders, the Taliban government is one of the few that recognize the independence of Chechniya.[3] Consequently, Russia provides direct and indirect aid, by means of the Russian army and military equipment, to CIS republics struggling against infiltration of fundamentalist Islamic influences and Islamic terror.[4]

Russian involvement is ensured by military agreements that obligate Russia to provide military aid to CIS republics in the event of an external threat.

- **The USA** – did not favor the establishment of extremist Islamic states or expansion of extremist Islamic influences to the Muslim republics of central Asia but, in 1996, did not see the Taliban as a tangible threat to American interests in the region. There were those who even found reasons to support the Taliban, although temporarily.[5]

The USA's primary concern was achieving calm and stability in the region and ending the civil war in Afghanistan. This goal was commensurate with extensive regional economic projects, including the laying of a pipeline through Afghanistan that would carry oil from the Muslim republics in Central Asia to Pakistan.[6]

Like Saudi Arabia, the USA wanted to use the Taliban – which was hostile to Iran and worked against its interests – to apply pressure on Iran. The USA even hoped that a stable regime in Afghanistan would facilitate future signing of agreements to prevent the export of opium and heroin and uproot international terror bases that had sprouted in Afghanistan under the auspices of the rival Mujahidin movements.

Nevertheless, there were a number of serious issues that prevented the development of relations between the USA and Afghanistan:

- Serious human rights infractions in Afghanistan under the Taliban, which were severely condemned by all international human rights organizations and inside the USA.
- The sanctuary Afghanistan gave to the terrorist Osama Bin Laden after the attacks he carried out against the USA embassies in Kenya and Tanzania.

In response to the attacks the USA bombed Bin Laden training facilities in Afghanistan and demanded his extradition from the Taliban regime. The Taliban however refused and even demanded that the USA apologize for the infraction on its sovereignty.[7]

The Taliban authorities gave Osama Bin Laden asylum and developed overtly anti-American rhetoric and propaganda.

After the "Monica Lewinsky scandal" became public Mohammed Omar, leader of the Taliban, declared that President Clinton was a corrupt individual deserving of the death penalty according to Taliban law.

Tension mounted between the Taliban regime and the USA around the latter's demand for the extradition of Bin Laden and improved protection of human rights in Afghanistan, culminating in the acute crisis caused by the new wave of terror that Bin Laden is accused of perpetrating and the USA's resolute demand for his extradition.

- **India** – supported Najibullah's Marxist regime during the civil war in Afghanistan and since its fall has maintained a holding pattern, observing events in Afghanistan without taking a stance. Its main interest is in preventing the spread of Islamic fundamentalism of the Afghan variety to the Kashmir region.

In 1993 it emerged that 1,000 Mujahidin warriors from Hekmatyar's movement had joined extremist Islamic elements in Kashmir. This move led to secret cooperation between India and Rabbani's regime in an attempt to work together against Hekmatyar.

The upheaval that occurred in the internal Afghan arena with the fall of the Rabbani regime and the rise of the Taliban resulted in a change in relations between India and the Afghan regime.

In 1999 Afghan soldiers, together with Islamic elements from Kashmir that were supported by Pakistan, invaded a number of areas in the Kashmir strip. India located the infiltration and launched an extensive military campaign that almost resulted in full scale war with Pakistan.

After several weeks of severe fighting India managed to repel the invaders from Kashmir but the tension between India and Pakistan and Afghanistan endured.

The Taliban government accused India of cooperating with Russia to help Masud's forces in their resistance to the Taliban.[8]

Pakistan – Afghanistan (Taliban) Relations

During the war between the Mujahidin and the Soviets Pakistan provided a base for the transfer of supplies, equipment, arms and money to the Mujahidin movements and the primary refuge for some four million Afghan refugees who fled there.

During the war Pakistan nurtured a number of Mujahidin movements in the hope that at the end of the struggle with the Soviets they would establish a friendly regime in Kabul that would serve Pakistani regional interests.

Hekmatyar and his extremist movement (Hizb-e-Islami) were among the main proteges of the Pakistanis who felt that this extremist Sunni movement based on the Pashtun majority in Afghanistan would have the best chances of establishing Islamic rule in Afghanistan.

After the Soviets were expelled from Afghanistan and Kabul fell into the hands of the Mujahidin, Pakistan supported the founding of a government wherein all Mujahidin factions would be represented, with Hekmatyar's movement and a number of other (pro-Pakistani) Mujahidin movements having the deciding weight. Pakistan's protege Hekmatyar, despite the offer to serve as prime minister in Mujadeddi's transitional government and later in Rabbani's, refused to cooperate and embarked on a military campaign on the assumption that he would be able to defeat his political and military rivals.

Hekmatyar's struggle against the Rabbani government led to a continuation of the civil war; because he did not manage to achieve any resolution, conflicts of interest soon arose between him and his patrons in Islamabad.

The ongoing civil war prevented the return of some four million Afghan refugees from Pakistan, who posed an economic burden for Pakistan and were a conduit for extremist political influences. Many Afghan refugees were arms or drug dealers and political rivalry between various Afghan groups often spilled over into violence and mutual casualties between Afghan refugees in Pakistan.

The Peshawar region on the border with Afghanistan became a breeding ground for Islamic terror organizations that recruited Muslim volunteers who had participated in the war against the Russians and afterward found themselves unemployed. Therefore the Pakistani government had a manifest interest in achieving quiet and stability in Afghanistan and solving the Afghan refugee problem on its own territory.

Hekmatyar's war with the Rabbani government also caused tension in relations between the Pakistan and Afghanistan governments, and despite Pakistan's denial of any involvement in the civil war it was clear beyond any doubt to the Rabbani government that Hekmatyar continued to receive Pakistani aid. Pakistan aspired to a settlement in Afghanistan as soon as possible, both so that it would be possible to use its territory as a bridge for forging economic relations with Muslim countries in central Asia and especially for laying an oil and gas pipeline from Turkmenistan to Pakistan, which was desperately in need of energy resources. Such a project could not be implemented as long as Afghanistan was in the midst of a civil war.

It was during 1993-1994 that the Pakistani government appears to have reached the conclusion that its protege Hekmatyar not only was incapable of attaining significant achievements in the Afghan political and military system, but was even causing damage to Pakistani interests, while Pakistan's ability to control him and dictate his moves was deteriorating.

At this stage it seems that Pakistan decided to cultivate the Taliban movement as the main source of power in the Afghan arena.

The Taliban movement, which had first made its appearance in Afghanistan in October 1994, initially destroyed the power and influence of Hekmatyar, probably on Pakistani orders, or at the very least with Pakistani agreement. During 1995-1996 Pakistan provided the Taliban with money, arms and Pakistani volunteers recruited to help it fight against the Rabbani government.[1]

In June 1996 this support led to a complete rupture in relations between the Rabbani and Pakistani governments, with the latter being accused of involvement in internal Afghan affairs.

In September 1996 after Kabul was conquered by the Taliban, it came as no surprise when the Pakistani government was the first to recognize the Taliban government as the legal government of Afghanistan.[2]

Pakistan was the main source of aid to the Taliban regime, providing military aid in its attempts to defeat the opposition and at the same time working politically toward a diplomatic settlement that will end the civil war and establish Taliban rule, with certain concessions made to the other ethnic minorities.

Pakistani mediators were working to mediate between the rival sides with recent attempts being made to convene a reconciliation conference in Islamabad with the participation of the rival sides and Pakistan and Iran as their patrons. (See reference to this in the chapter on diplomatic steps to settle the conflict in Afghanistan.)

In the UN Pakistan worked to achieve recognition for the Taliban government, proposing a compromise whereby the seat reserved for the Afghan representative and which was still occupied by a representative of the Rabbani government would be frozen until an internal settlement is reached in Afghanistan.[3]

Pakistan, which suffers from grave ethnically-based internal problems, lack of political stability, and an ongoing conflict with India, is interested in achieving stability on its western border which will lead to the return of over four million Afghan refugees that are resident in its Peshawar region.[4]

Despite Pakistan's support for the Taliban movement, there are many groups in Pakistan that view the extremist Islamic regime taking shape in neighboring Afghanistan – which is the source of inspiration for Islamic fundamentalist groups in Pakistan itself – with suspicion.

The Taliban movement supported by the Pakistani government tried to implement a political and ideological structure that is significantly different from the secular regimes that have characterized Pakistan (both civilian regimes such as Benazir Bhutto's and military regimes such as the present one).

For this reason there are groups in Pakistan that fear that the end of the civil war in Afghanistan and Taliban victory might cause the "monster to rise up against his creator," with the Taliban becoming a tangible threat to the secular regime in Pakistan. These groups would prefer a peace settlement in Afghanistan that would enable the various components of the opposition to be included in the regime and thus constitute a stabilizing and restraining factor on the Taliban's extremist orientation.[5]

Iran – Afghanistan (Taliban) Relations

The Taliban movement differs from most Afghan Mujahidin movements and also from most Islamic movements active in Muslim countries. It is not satisfied with having taken control and expelled an Islamic regime that according to its ideology had failed to realize the notion of the establishment of a proper Islamic state, but strives to apply a specific, extremist Islamic interpretation. The Taliban is hence part of the religious and ideological Islamic movements that sought to bring about genuine reform in Islam.

The Taliban to a large extent constitute a protest against Shiite Islam based on the model of the Islamic state determined by Shiite Iran.

For close to fifteen years Iran has provided a symbol and model of Islamic fundamentalism, almost the only example of a radical Islamic state.

Khomeini and his successors aspired to downplay the contradictions between Shiite and Sunni in the spirit of ecumenical understanding and the right to religious legitimacy and recognition among the Sunni as well. This effort was relatively unsuccessful because of Shiite Iran's unique and distinct position in the central stream of the Sunni Muslim world.

The Taliban movement, unlike Islamic movements such as the Muslim Brotherhood or the even the more radical Islamic Jihad organizations who are willing to draw nearer to and be aided by Iran and even adopt elements of its ideology as a model, is hostile to Iran and Shiite Islam, and is once again exacerbating the Sunni-Shiite conflict on the ground.

An expression of their hostility to the Shiites can be observed in the prohibition of celebration of the Persian new year.

Foreign agencies report that Shiite religious officials were warned by the

Taliban not to celebrate the Persian new year, and Shiite residents of Kabul who were caught disobeying this regulation were severely beaten by members of the Taliban. The Taliban's message is therefore directed from a Sunni Islamic reform movement at the entire Muslim nation, unlike Khomeini's doctrine which is the result of a minority trying to influence and illuminate the majority.

Iran thus perceives the Taliban not only as a threat to local interests in the Afghan arena, but also as an ideological and religious threat to their very status in the Muslim world.

The Taliban's success in establishing their rule and founding an Islamic state in the "Taliban spirit" in Afghanistan is likely to be a source of inspiration and a model for emulation among other radical Islamic movements which have seen Iran as the only model that succeeded in doing so.

The hostility between Iran and the Taliban is reflected in the military, economic and diplomatic aid that Iran supplies to the opposition forces struggling against the Taliban regime in Afghanistan. Throughout the years of the struggle against the Marxist regime Iran supplied aid to the Shiite minority in Afghanistan (the Hazars).

After the Taliban came to power the opposition organized itself on an ethnic national basis which included the Tajikis, Uzbekis, Hazaras and others. This opposition received massive aid from Russia and Iran, who sought to protect the interests of the minorities they supported and also in order to block the spread of Taliban-style radical Islam.

Against the background of Iranian support for the opposition, and following the kidnapping and murder of Iranian diplomats in Afghanistan, Iran went so far as to threaten military action against the Taliban. This never materialized, but the tension and hostility endured. Saudi Arabia and some of the Gulf states see the Taliban as a new and effective tool in their struggle against Iran. Their support for the Taliban, mainly expressed in financial support and political recognition of the legitimacy of the regime, reveals their conviction that at least in the short term, Taliban success will be a source of pressure on Iran and help introduce Saudi influences into the Muslim republics in central Asia.

Saudi Arabia seems unaware of the danger that in the long term the Taliban could become a "double-edged sword" against the Saudi regime, its pro-Western lifestyle, behavior and policies which are in absolute contradistinction to the puritanical world view of the Taliban.

Diplomatic Moves to Resolve the Conflict in Afghanistan 1993-2000

Very little was done to stop the battles and attain peace and stability in Afghanistan
between 1993-1996. There were however, three main initiatives during this time that warrant mentioning: one by the UN, the second by the Union of Muslim Countries and the third by President Rabbani.

At the start of 1994 the secretary general of the UN appointed a special emissary, Mohammed Mastiri (from Tunisia). Mastiri visited Afghanistan and the neighboring countries in April, August and September of 1994 in an attempt to formulate agreements for a cease-fire and political settlement in Afghanistan. The UN secretary general Boutrous Ghali also came to Pakistan in September 1994 and met with representatives of all the Afghan Mujahidin movements in an attempt to formulate agreements.

In October 1994, UN emissary Mastiri submitted a proposal for resolution of the conflict in Afghanistan. The plan included the following components:

Declaration of a multilateral cease-fire.

Establishment of a transitional council that would include representatives of the government, opposition movements, neutral representatives and UN representatives. The council would function as a temporary government for 6-12 months until the convention of traditional leaders (Jirga) or elections.

Another alternative proposed was that the transitional council would act **immediately** after convening to bring about the Jirga or hold presidential elections at once.

The UN emissary's proposals did not receive the blessing of any of the sides in Afghanistan and the mediation initiative faded, with the UN maintaining its presence in Afghanistan by means of 3 offices (in Herat, Kandahar and Jalalabad) that dealt mainly in humanitarian aid.

In July 1994 the Union of Muslim States made a mediation attempt in the conflict in Afghanistan. The organization's secretary Hamed el Jabid visited Kabul and met with President Rabbani.

Hekmatyar reacted to the mediation initiative with a barrage of rockets fired at the presidential palace in Kabul while President Rabbani was meeting with the mediator. This mediation attempt also failed and since then this organization has not renewed its efforts.

In July 1994 President Rabbani initiated a meeting in the city of Herat, to which all the Mujahidin leaders and veteran political figures were invited to attend.

Some 700 dignitaries from among Rabbani's supporters attended but all the opposition movements were absent. At the meeting President Rabbani called for a broad traditional convention of leaders in Afghanistan (Loya Jirga) in order to reach an agreement about the future political structure of the country.

At the close of the convention it was decided to appoint a committee that would be charged with working to convene the Jirga on October 23, 1994. The decision to establish a national army that would number 100,000 men and that would collect arms from the militias in order to restore public security and order in the country was also taken.

President Rabbani's initiative was rejected by all the opposition movements and the Jirga that was intended to clarify the political settlement issues was never convened.

Subsequent to the fall of Rabbani's regime and the rise of the Taliban, the opposing sides in the Afghan civil war changed. The "Northern Alliance" front headed by the Tajikis Rabbani and Sheikh Masud, the Uzbeki General Dostum, the Shiite Hizb-e-Wahadat and the remnants of Hekmatyar's forces formed in opposition to the central government headed by the Taliban, which controls most of Afghanistan's territory.

Various parties have made renewed attempts to mediate a peace agreement between the rival sides in Afghanistan since 1996; among these, the following initiatives are of note:

- In September 1996, an emissary of the UN Secretary General met with the Taliban leaders to negotiate a cease-fire and initiate UN-sponsored peace talks.[1]

- In 1996 there was an initiative to convene a peace conference in Islamabad with the participation of the rival Afghan sides, the countries supporting one of the sides: Pakistan, Iran, Tajikistan, Turkmenistan, Uzbekistan, and the USA and Russia as observers. Despite intensive efforts with the help of the UN, the initiative failed.
- In 1997 there was an Uzbeki peace initiative led by the Uzbeki foreign minister who even presented this plan to the UN. It, too, failed.[2]
- In 1998 there was a Pakistani attempt at mediation in order to achieve a cease-fire for the month of Ramadan as a first stage and later to hold peace talks. The proposal was rejected by the Taliban on the grounds that a cease-fire was a "ruse" to enable the opposition to stand firm.[3]
- Other Pakistani efforts were made during 1999 in meetings between the President of Iran Khatemi and the Prime Minister of Pakistan Nawaz Sharif that were held at the Islamic conference in Teheran, and later during meetings between the foreign ministers of the two countries. None of these efforts were successful.[4]
- In 1999 the president of Turkmenistan attempted a mediation effort with the help of a UN emissary. In talks representatives of the rival sides expressed their willingness to reach a peace agreement, but eventually this bid also failed like those preceding it.[5]

So far, it appears that the ceaseless efforts by various countries and international organizations to bring about the end of the civil war in Afghanistan and achieve a peace agreement have been ineffective, and the war continues.[6]

"Afghan Terror" in the International Arena as a Reflection of Cultural Conflict

In the summer of 1993 Professor Samuel Huntington, a lecturer in international affairs at Harvard University, published an article entitled "The Clash of Civilizations."[1] The article generated waves in the international academic community. Professor Huntington continued his work in the wake of the scholastic polemics it raised and in 1996 published a book that bore the same title.[2]

Professor Huntington argues that the root of conflicts in the world at the end of the 20th century and the beginning of the next millennium are neither ideological nor economic, but first and foremost cultural. He claims that four stages can be observed in the development of conflicts in the modern world:[3]

- **The first stage** – Conflicts used to be between princes and kings, based on rivalries and personal interests and the desire to obtain economic assets and expand the area under their control.
- **The second stage** – Since the French Revolution and the emergence of nationalism, conflicts have been between nations rather than kings and princes or, in Huntington's words, "The wars of kings are over, the wars of people had begun."[4]

  This stage reached its historical end after World War I.
- **The third stage** – Since the rise of Communism in Russia conflicts have been between competing ideologies, first between Communism and fascism and

democratic liberalism, and later between Communism and democratic liberalism (the "Cold War" or "East against West").
- **The fourth stage** – (the present one) – The period since the end of the "Cold War" has been marked by conflicts between cultures.

Huntington claims that until the end of the Cold War the world was dominated by Western culture and most of the significant clashes that took place were within this cultural rubric of what he calls "Western civil wars."[5]

At the end of the Cold War era the international political system broke free of the domination of Western culture, and the center of gravity instead became reciprocal relations and conflicts between the West and non-Western cultures and between non-Western cultures and other non-Western cultures.

From this stage on, nations and peoples belonging to non-Western civilizations stopped being the products of influence and the victims of Western colonialism and became active, dominant partners in propelling and designing history.

During the Cold War the world was categorized according to political systems and countries' economic and technological development. (Developed and developing countries, first, second and third world countries, etc.)

Huntington avers that today countries are classified by culture or civilization. According to this definition "a civilization is the highest cultural grouping of people and the broadest level of cultural identity people have short of that which distinguishes humans from others."[6]

Civilization is defined by means of objective components, such as language, history, religion, customs, and institutions, and by subjective components like self-definition or the individual's identification with a group.

It can therefore be said that the civilization with which the individual is identified is the one that constitutes the broadest and deepest level of cultural identification for him.

Huntington numbers eight key civilizations in the modern world: Western, Slavic, Chinese-Confucian, Japanese, Hindi, Latin-American, Islamic, and African.[7] He cites Islamic civilization as the most militant in our times and as inherently in a state of conflict with Western culture and with other cultures as well.

Huntington points out the historical roots of this conflict which began with the Crusades and continued through the Ottoman Empire, Western colonialism and the Muslim countries' wars of liberation.

A brief glance at the map of conflicts in the world provides convincing testament to Huntington's arguments. From Africa in the west to the Pacific ocean islands, Islam is engaged in violent conflicts along the lines of contact or friction with other civilizations (fault line wars).

By way of example Huntington cites the following conflicts:

- The Afghanistan war.
- The Gulf war.
- The war between the Bosnians and the Serbs.
- The conflict between the Serbs and Albanians.[8]
- The conflict between Turkey and Greece.
- Ethnic and religious conflicts in the former Soviet Union.
- The war between Azerbaijan and Armenia.

A more current picture, as of the year 2000, only reinforces Huntington's claims with further evidence:

- The civil war between Christians and Muslims in the Sudan.
- The war between Christian Ethiopia and Muslim Eritrea.
- The war in Kosovo between the Christian Serbs and the Muslim Albanians.
- The war in Chechnya and Daghastan and the subversion of the pro-Russian regimes in Tajikistan and Uzbekistan.
- The continued conflict with Iraq.
- The war between India and Pakistan over Kashmir.
- Subversive activity of nationalist Ulghur Muslims in western China.
- The struggle between Muslims and the Christian regime in the Philippines for control of Mindanao (Moro).
- The war between Muslim Indonesians and Christians in East Timor.
- The Israeli-Arab conflict, which is a significant component in the conflicts between Islam and Western culture.

Although the political reality does bolster Huntington's overall perception, some of his arguments should be critiqued and circumscribed.

Huntington offers a sweeping, comprehensive approach that represents all Muslim nations as one Islamic cultural entity in confrontation with Western culture and other cultures. A close examination of the regimes in most Muslim countries shows that the majority of them are secular or have moderate, pragmatic Islamic orientations and that they are not in conflict with the West but rather have taken the band-wagon approach and joined the ranks of modernization, adopting Western technologies, values and lifestyles.

Huntington does not distinguish between this central stream in the Muslim world and the fundamentalist Islamic stream, which does indeed make conflict with Western culture its aim but which is still a militant minority in the Muslim world.

The Muslim world, therefore, is beset by a deep and severe internal cultural conflict over the nature and path of Muslim society, and the results of this internal struggle dictate, and will continue to dictate, the nature of relations between Islamic culture and Western and other cultures.

The regimes in many Muslim countries have not only adopted Western cultural patterns but even rely on Western military, political and economic aid to survive.

Radical Islamic streams exist and operate at various levels of intensity and violence in all Muslim countries, also towards attaining independence for the Muslim minorities in countries identified with other cultures (China, the Philippines, Serbia, India, etc.).

The objective of these elements is to bring about the establishment of Islamic religious states by replacing the secular regimes in Muslim countries, attaining independence for Muslim communities in countries where they are minorities and establishing new Islamic states.

Radical Islam is therefore involved in a struggle against foreign cultures on four levels:

- Replacing secular regimes in Muslim countries with Islamic regimes.
- The struggle of Muslim minorities to obtain independence and establish independent Islamic states.
- The struggle against ethnic/cultural minorities demanding autonomy or independence from Islamic states.
- The struggle against foreign cultures, especially Western culture, along the lines of contact and friction with Islamic culture.

This reality is commensurate with the basic assumption of Islam that sees the world as divided into Islamic territory (Dar el Islam) and war territory (Dar el Harb), with the goal of Islam being to bring true faith to all human civilizations. Islamic fundamentalism employs a variety of means and tools in the service of achieving its goals – from education, publicity, financial aid, and spiritual support, to political subversion, terror and war.

Analysis of the foci of the conflict shows that the efforts of Islamic fundamentalists are directed first and foremost at changing the political reality within the Muslim world and to a lesser degree in relation to other cultures.

The radical Islamic elements include three countries whose regimes can be characterized as fundamentalist Islamic regimes – Iran, Afghanistan and the Sudan – as well as dozens of fundamentalist Islamic organizations that are active throughout the Muslim world.

Fundamentalist Islamic states are a source of inspiration, encouragement, funding, and support for the radical Islamic movements and work both independently and through these movements to export their brand of Islamic revolution and struggle against foreign cultures, especially Western culture.

Three events or processes in the last millennium had a decisive impact on the development of Islamic fundamentalism:

- The Khomeini revolution in Iran – Turning Iran into a focus of radical Islam, exporting the revolution to the Muslim world and raising radical Islam's complaint against the superpowers' hegemony under the slogan "not East and not West."
- The victory of the Islamic Mujahidin in Afghanistan – The defeat of the Soviet Union in battle was perceived by Muslim groups as not only a victory of Islam on the battlefield but also a victory of cultural values which resulted in the creation of a broad cadre of volunteers inflamed with Islamic fervor and battle experience who would work toward the continued dissemination of fundamentalist Islamic ideas.
- The fall of the Soviet Union and the collapse of Communist ideology – Creating a political and ideological void that provided a historical "window of opportunity" for Islamic groups.

The Communism and socialism that were the ideological basis for a significant number of the secular regimes in Muslim countries collapsed, and an ideological vacuum was created which radical Islam is trying to penetrate, thus far with only partial success.

The dissolution of the Soviet empire led to the emergence of new countries with Muslim populations that constitute a new theater of action for Islamic groups.

For the first time in decades the question of the Muslim identity of the Baltic populations (Bosnia, Kosovo, Albania) arose in Europe, and religious and ethnic conflicts present an opportunity for the ideological ideas of extremist Islam to gain a foothold.

The new geopolitical reality in the post-cold war era is perceived by radical Islamic groups as a reflection of their success and puts Islam at the forefront of the conflict with Western culture, with the USA – the only superpower – at its center. One of the prominent phenomena of the end of the last millennium and the beginning of the current one which clearly reflects Huntington's notion of cultural conflict is the "Afghan" phenomenon, which has become the spearhead of radical Islamic confrontation with rival cultures.

"Afghan" terrorists, despite the appellation, are not identified with and do not belong to a specific movement or country but reflect a radical cultural stream that advocates the uncompromising struggle of Islam against impious Muslim regimes and rival cultures.

International Terror – Theoretical Background

Since the 1970s, in the wake of international terrorist activity and the need to understand and cope with the phenomenon, a research discipline has developed, mainly in Western democratic countries, that examines the question of terrorism from various angles, such as the legal, psychological, sociological, and historical aspects, and other domains of political science. The attention paid to terrorism today is accompanied by researchers' basic frustration because reaching a universal definition of the phenomenon has proved difficult. This is not because scholars are unable to define terror, but because they are unable to settle on one definition acceptable to all from among the many that have been formulated .

There are various ways to distinguish between different categories of definition. One such distinction is between normative definitions and analytical definitions.[1] Conor Cruise O'Brien is one of the representatives of the normative approach. His definitions are based on political values from which he derives criteria for judging political activity. O'Brien defines terrorism in terms of the political contexts in which it occurs, and defines it as "unjustified violence against a democratic state which permits effective modes of non-violent opposition."[2] One of the main limitations of this normative definition is the subjective aspect of the phenomenon, by which an ally or friend is defined positively (freedom fighter) while a rival is defined as a "terrorist." For this reason it is difficult to define the term terror in a clear, universal manner on the basis of the normative definition.

The importance and advantage of normative definitions is actually in positing the question of the legitimacy of the use of political violence as a criterion for judgment.

Anthony Quinton makes a key point on the question of legitimacy, arguing: "The key to a country's coping with terror is defending the legitimacy of its use of violence and denying the legitimacy of the terrorist challenge."[3] To a large degree, the aim of terror is the attempt to acquire legitimation from the population (or part of it) and to deny the regime its legitimacy. O'Brien defined this well: "Terrorism challenges the rights of the regime to have a monopoly over power in the society and physically weakens its ability to maintain law and order."[4]

Other questions that emerge from the normative approach deal with the moral aspects of terror. Martha Crenshaw argues that terrorism can be judged from two perspectives: examining the morality of the results, and examining the morality of the means. In terms of the results of terror activity, the touchstone is whether the goal of the activity is to establish a just regime of equality and freedom or to serve the narrow, proscribed goals of establishing a regime of inequality that will give added rights to a defined group while denying human freedoms.

Discussing the morality of the means leads to an examination of the methods and means that terror employs, in particular the question of the victims' identity. Crenshaw defines two main groups of victims: the first group includes individuals who are vulnerable to terror activity because of the positions they occupy and the fact that they are identified to a greater or lesser degree with the "wicked" policy the terrorists are fighting against; the other includes citizens of the country who do not hold public office, or the citizens of other countries that have no connections with or direct influence on the government policy. The "sin" of these citizens, in the eyes of terrorists, is their obeisance to the laws of an "unjust" regime, which makes them accessories to its deeds.

The question of victims of terror is another example of why normative definitions are problematic. The observer's perspective is what really determines his moral attitude to a particular incident. It seems therefore that an objective moral judgment of the use of terror in different political circumstances is unattainable, and the most that can be said is that defining an action as "terrorist" is not a moral value judgment of its essence.

While the normative school tries to deal with the term "terror" through examining normative ethical values, the analytical school tries to find the formula for defining the phenomenon by constructing a neutral theoretical definition that will be comprehensive enough to address the spectrum of variations of terror.

One of the most comprehensive studies of the subject was done by Alex

Schmidt.[5] His study is based on the assumption that despite lack of agreement with regard to the definition of terror, there is a common denominator to the images usually associated with terror and this agreement is clear enough to construct a model that will be a common language for scholars of terror. Schmidt collected one hundred and nine different definitions of terror and performed a "content analysis" of them in an attempt to locate the elements common to them. His findings show twenty-two similar elements, the most prominent of which are: employment of violence/force (appeared in 83.5 of the definitions), political goals (in 95%), spreading of fear (in 51%), threat and application of psychological pressure (in 47%), attention to the difference between terror victims (in 37.5%), systematic and/or planned activity (in 32%).

The list of parameters or components that Schmidt arrived at is not enough to provide a real definition of the phenomenon, but his work makes it possible to identify the central components related to terrorism, and Schmidt tried to construct his definition of terror on this basis.[6] According to Schmidt, terrorism is a system of attack where incidental or symbolic victims are instrumental targets for violence. The victims are distinguished by group characteristics that are the basis for their being selected as victims. The prior use of violence, or a proven threat of the use of violence, makes other members of the target group into victims because of the "chronic fear" they experience. This indirect kind of attack is meant to make the victims act in accordance with the terrorists' wishes or to cause secondary targets to change their approaches or behaviors in accordance with the terrorists' goals.[7] Schmidt's comprehensive approach contributed to understanding the phenomenon and mapping of the components common to the different definitions, but he, too, was unable to generate a universal definition of the phenomenon. The failure to reach a universal definition of the phenomenon of terror also dogs the research into the "derivatives" of terror, such as international terror and "state-supported" terror.

In the 1970s, attempts were made at two research institutions in the US to define international terror. The first was performed at the Rand Institute where researchers defined international terrorism as:

> An isolated incident or series of incidents in contravention of the accepted law, diplomatic settlements and the law of warfare. International terror is meant to attract international attention to the existence of the problem the terrorists are struggling against, and to sow fear. The aim of terror is to cause an effect or change according to the wishes of its perpetrators, with the direct victim not necessarily identical to the element the terror is trying to influence.[8]

The researchers of the Interate Project reached a different definition of international terror, which holds that terror is:

> The use of violence, or the threat of the use of violence, for political goals by an individual or group working on behalf of or against an existing regime. The act is meant to influence the widest possible target population of direct victims, with the victims, the perpetrators or their contacts crossing borders.[9]

The various kinds of state involvement in terror were grouped under the concepts "terrorist states" or "state-sponsored terrorism."

These concepts include the various degrees of state involvement in terror, and more focussed assessment is required, therefore, in order to classify states' involvement in terror according to the following categories:[10]

- **States supporting terrorism** – This category includes states that support terrorist organizations by means of financial, ideological, military, and operational aid.
- **States operating terrorism** – States that initiate, direct and execute terror activities through the patronage of organizations (while refraining from the direct involvement of government bodies in terror).
- **States perpetrating terror** – States that perpetrate terror all over the world by means of state security systems (security and intelligence mechanisms).

Paul Wilkinson defined the various kinds of state terror as the "direct or indirect involvement of a government, by means of formal or informal groups, in creating psychological and physical violence against political targets or another state for the purpose of achieving tactical and strategic goals."[11]

"State terror is characterized by a double standard towards international law and order on the one hand – states that use terror are willing to deviate from international norms and the "rules of the game" in order to harm a rival and achieve their objectives (a prominent example of this was the "student" taking over the US embassy in Iran and taking diplomats hostage in 1979) – and on the other hand the state using terror tries not to expose its involvement in this activity in order to prevent the victim from taking retaliatory action.[12]

Cooperation between the state and the terror organization is usually based on religious, ideological or political identification through common interests. The "patron's" degree of control over the terror organization varies according to the basis for cooperation and the organization's level of dependence on "patronage."

States' involvement in terror can be direct or indirect at various levels of aid and cooperation (moral, political, economic, operational). In most cases the connections between the "patron" state and the terror organizations are secretive and utilize citizens of other countries. This makes it easier for the state to disavow any responsibility should the activity be exposed and thereby avoid criticism and sanctions in the international system.[13]

Terror can be another aspect of, or alternative to, the operation of military forces in order to achieve the state's objectives when the state supports a terror activity against a state with which it is at war. It can also be used between states that are not formally hostile to one another.

Terror can be effective in achieving objectives that direct military confrontation would not necessarily realize, such as political destabilization in the target country or damage to diplomatic or economic ties with other countries.[14]

"Cultural Terror"

"Cultural terror" is a form of international terror that makes a cultural object the target of an act of terror. From this perspective cultural terror can be analyzed using both the Rand and the Interate Institutes' definitions.

The Rand Institute defined international terror as follows:[1]

"An isolated incident or series of incidents in contravention of the accepted law, diplomatic settlements and the law of warfare. International terror is meant to attract international attention to the existence of the problem the terrorists are struggling against, and to sow fear. The aim of terror is to cause an effect or change according to the wishes of its perpetrators, with the direct victim not necessarily identical to the element the terror is trying to influence."

Damage or the threat of damage to a cultural or religious asset is, of course, a contravention of diplomatic agreements and the laws of war. Cultural assets, and certainly holy sites, are perceived in international law and norms of behavior to enjoy special status and protection even during times of war.

Damage to a "cultural asset" is first and foremost a serious injury to the state where the asset is located, and because "cultural assets" usually have importance for populations wider than the direct population of the state, terror against such a target presents the state and its rulers as incapable of ensuring the protection of the assets they are entrusted with. This brings a network of extensive external pressures to bear in order to improve the authorities' readiness to take action that would prevent damage to the asset. "Cultural terror" therefore creates extremely wide resonance among the media, which focuses world attention on the issue the terrorists want to put on the agenda.

The direct victim of terror, in this case the "cultural object," can be identified with or essential to the entity that the terror is trying to affect, but there is also the possibility that the cultural object is located in a certain state but is not identified with it culturally. (For example archeological or religious sites that are more important to populations outside the countries where they are located.)

The Interate Institute defines international terror as:[2]

"The use of violence, or the threat of the use of violence, for political goals by an individual or group working on behalf of or against an existing regime. The act is meant to influence the widest possible target population of direct victims, with the victims, the perpetrators or their contacts crossing borders."

"Cultural terror" is by definition a crossing of boundaries that is intended to affect the widest possible target population.

The perpetrators of the act of terror may act on behalf of a certain regime or sometimes even be part of its operational mechanisms (state terror), or alternatively may work against the regime through acts of terror designed to harm it and destabilize its legitimacy.

"Cultural terror" can be part of a conflict between states (anything from a limited clash to a full scale war), or between a terror organization and a state, or as part of community disputes within states (the most extreme instance being civil war).

"Cultural terror" can also be the impetus for expanding a local, limited conflict into a broad cultural one, carrying along with it states and organizations that ostensibly were not involved into the original dispute.

In many instances cultural terror results in the equivalence of the cultural and religious components of the conflict. Afghanistan is a clear example of a country that uses cultural terror, and the destruction of the statues of Buddha in Bamian illustrates this phenomenon clearly.

Destruction of the Statues of Buddha at Bamian – Afghanistan – 2001

In February 2001 Mullah Mohammed Omar, leader of the Taliban, decided to launch a campaign to "culturally cleanse" Afghanistan of influences from foreign cultures – especially cultures identified with idol worship.

The Afghan minister of publicity explained:

"Our religious sages issued an incontrovertible religious edict according to which statues have no place in a Muslim country."[1]

Two giant statues of Buddha carved into the rock in Bamian, some two hundred and thirty kilometers west of the capital Kabul, were selected as the main target of this "cultural cleansing" campaign. The two statues were sculpted into the rock during the third and fifth centuries CE:[2]

- A statue of a male, 53 meters high (the highest statue of Buddha in the world).
- A statue of a female, 36 meters high.

Bamian lies on the historical "Silk Road" that facilitated commercial ties between China and the Roman empire. Historically Bamian was a center of Buddhist cultural development. Many Buddhist monks lived there and the place became a site of pilgrimage for many of that faith.

The giant statues of Buddha survived all historical upheavals, and during the civil war that took place in Afghanistan from 1979-1992, and even afterwards, the warring sides were careful not to damage the statues because of their cultural and archeological importance. The Taliban movement that has controlled most of the territory of Afghanistan since 1994 is the most extreme instance of radical Sunni Islam, and the movement's leaders made it their mission to establish a religious Islamic state that would function according to the Taliban's strict interpretation of Shariah and the Muslim ways of life derived from it, as well as wage an uncompromising struggle against corrupting cultures "from the East and West."[3]

Afghanistan's "cultural cleansing" of foreign cultures and influences faithfully reflects the Taliban world view, which sees Islam as immersed in an existential struggle to save and preserve its authentic culture.

This perception was expressed in the movement's early days in its policy towards Afghan society and foreign states and cultures.

Immediately after the decision to destroy the statues became public, the international community rallied in an attempt to save the Buddhas.[4]

Many countries, the US, Germany, France (which are associated with Western culture), most Buddhist countries including India and Thailand, and even Muslim countries like Pakistan, Malaysia and Iran, called on the Taliban to refrain from harming the statues.

The Metropolitan Museum in New York and other museums in Europe offered to buy the statues from the Taliban and transport them out of Afghanistan, but to no avail.[5]

The Taliban tried for two weeks to destroy the statues using cannon fire and missiles and after these methods did not work they blew them up with explosives.[6]

Taliban leader Mullah Mohammed Omar ordered the slaughter of 100 cows throughout the country as a sacrifice in order to ask forgiveness for the two-week delay in destroying the statues. The meat of the slaughtered cows was distributed as charity to the poor throughout the country.[7]

When the statues' destruction was complete, the Taliban made sure to transport foreign journalists from Kabul to the site in order to report the event.

Afghanistan was then hit with a furious wave of protest from around the world, especially from irate Buddhist masses who called for revenge. In India stormy demonstrations took place in which Buddhist adherents burned copies of the Koran.[8]

The destruction of the Buddha statues in Afghanistan, or the "Bamian Massacre" as it is called in Buddhist circles, raised many question marks about the move and its timing.[9]

The Taliban saw fit to make public, first, the decision to destroy the statues – which generated intense international pressure – and later the actual destruction, which invoked condemnation and protest throughout the world.

Taliban spokesmen provided no explanations for this other than stating that "this is a question of Muslim religious law and a religious commandment."[10]

This act of "cultural terror" perpetrated by the Taliban was apparently meant to convey the following messages:

- The Taliban are determined to implement their strict interpretation of Islamic law and give it public expression so that it serves as a message and model for emulation.
- The Taliban wanted this act of "cultural terrorism" to expose the hypocrisy and "double standards" of the international network, especially the US.
  The Taliban claimed there was international willingness to offer significant financial resources to save the statues but that Afghanistan's appeals for humanitarian aid to save human lives in poor, battle-scarred Afghanistan were not answered.
- The "cultural terrorism" attack on the statues of Buddha was a Taliban diatribe against the international system, its laws and rules, and was meant to prove its helplessness.
  This appears to be the reason for their actions, namely, declaring in advance their intention to destroy the statues, which brought on an array of applications and requests and their refusal by the Taliban, while they emphasized their adherence to religious principles at all costs. The goal was destruction of the statues and presentation of the results for all the world to see, while emphasizing the helplessness of the international system to prevent the deed.
- The Bamian region is mainly inhabited by Shiites (Hazars) but despite the Muslim identity of the population the Buddha statues were part of the region's cultural, archeological and tourism assets.[11]
  Bamian and its surroundings were the scene of fierce battles between the Taliban and their rivals until the former conquered the region in 1998. Residents of the region are still suspected of identifying with enemies of the Taliban.
  Therefore the damage inflicted on the Buddha statues was also damage to this population and a signal of deterrence to the opposition working against the Taliban and its supporters (among them India with its Buddhist population).
- In the absence of significant "Western" cultural and religious symbols, the Buddha statues were the most overt and prominent example of a foreign culture on Afghan soil. Moreover, according to the history of Islam, members of the monotheistic religions were protected by Islam when under its wing, while Buddhism did not enjoy similar status.

Ancient Islam was hostile to Buddhism, with Muslims seeing Buddhists as "idol worshippers" and therefore persecuting them in regions under Islamic rule.

The Taliban, who adopt the most severe interpretations of Islamic religious law, see this as the continuation of a historical process that began in the days of the prophet Mohammed as part of the campaign to cleanse society of statues and idol worship.

In conclusion, it appears that at the root of the "cultural terror" act that led to destruction of the statues of Buddha in Bamian lay religious, religious-legal and political considerations as part of the Taliban's cultural struggle against foreign cultures (in this case the Indian-Buddhist culture) and the international system.

With this act of terror the Taliban sought to prove that should the international system continue to work against their regime, the Taliban can damage sensitive weak spots and expose the international system and the superpowers in all their vulnerability.

Destruction of the Statues of Buddha in Bamian

Afghan Terror in the International Arena

During the 1980s Afghanistan was a magnet for Muslim volunteers from various Muslim and Arab countries that came to the aid of the Afghan Mujahidin in their struggle against the pro-Soviet regime in Kabul and the Soviet invasion forces. There are no exact statistics on the number of volunteers, but apparently several thousand heeded the call of Afghan Jihad out of religious identification or a sense of adventure and avarice.[1] During their stay in Afghanistan the volunteers underwent military training and acquired rich combat experience in guerilla warfare.

The training of Mujahidin and their volunteers usually took place in Pakistan, with the city of Peshawar (near the Afghan border) and its environs being the center and focus of Mujahidin activity.[2] Training was provided by Pakistani instructors, experts from Arab countries and for a time also by Western experts, mainly from America.[3] In addition to the camps in Pakistan, volunteers from Arab countries also underwent training in camps in the Sudan, Yemen and Iran. We have no statistics on how the volunteers divided up according to their affiliations with the various Afghan rebels. The little that we do know indicates that Hekmatyar's extremist organization (Hizb-e-Islami) absorbed most of the volunteers (some reports say about 3,500 individuals) some of whom continue to serve in its ranks in the struggle against the Rabbani regime in Kabul.[4] After the fall of the pro-Soviet regime in Kabul (May 1992) the volunteers were no longer needed in Afghanistan and they began to return to their countries of origin.

Despite the Pakistani government's declaration in January 1993[5] that it intended to close the offices of the Afghan movements and deport all those who remained in its territory illegally, in practice nothing was done to implement the decision and many Mujahidin continued to reside in camps in Peshawar and other parts of the country as well.

Another category, called the "Afghan alumni," refers to the hundreds of members of Islamic terror organizations who came to Afghanistan after the end of the war and underwent training in guerilla warfare and terror under the various Mujahidin factions.

"Afghan alumni" are today a central component in the leadership of fundamentalist Islamic terror organizations, their status based on the ethos of heroic participation in the Jihad and their victory over the Soviet superpower, as well as their rich operational experience.

Four principle channels of "Afghan alumni" activity can be observed:

A. Involvement in the activities and management of radical Islamic organizations in their countries of origin (Egypt, the Maghreb, Jordan, etc.)
B. Establishment of new terror organizations such as Osama Bin Laden's Al Qaeda.
C. Establishment of "independent" terror cells with no affiliation to or connection with specific organizations, but which cooperate with other established terror organizations.
D. Joining in fighting by other Islamic populations, such as in Bosnia, Kosovo, Chechnya, Tajikistan, and Kashmir.

Although they usually went to Afghanistan with the blessing of their countries' regimes, their return met with energetic resistance from the authorities due to the fear the "Afghans" would quickly become a threat to the regimes themselves because of their military experience and fundamentalist world view.

For this reason, in most of the Maghreb countries, in Egypt and in Jordan, the authorities worked to prevent the volunteers' return and integration into the ranks of the radical Islamic oppositions in their own lands. One of the prominent leaders of the "Arab Afghans" is Ahmed Shauqi el Islambuli, the brother of President Sadat's assassin. In interviews el Islambuli and other radical leaders deny the definition of their activity as terror and claim that their actions to bring down "corrupt" regimes in Egypt, Algeria, Tunisia, and other places follow the format of Jihad which aims to change the nature of the regimes in these countries.[6]

Afghanistan, Sudan and even Yemen are today focal points of activity and havens and waystations for Afghan alumni on their way back to their countries of origin in order to join the ranks of radical Islamic movements there.

Iran, despite religious and ideological differences of opinion with Taliban

Afghanistan, is host to leaders of organizations affiliated with the Afghan alumni, supports a number of groups that identify with the Afghan alumni in Lebanon, and even facilitates passage of activists and weapons to the Mujahidin fighting in Chechnya.

Nevertheless Iran's caution and circumspection in regard to its connections with the Afghan alumni and the tension that characterizes its relations with Afghanistan must be emphasized.[7]

Algeria

During the 1980s there was an influx of volunteers from Algeria to Afghanistan, and between several hundred and three thousand men fought alongside the Afghan Mujahidin.[8] The Algerian Mujahidin in Afghanistan and Pakistan were divided during the struggle with the Soviets and remain divided still, into two streams – one that supports the radical Islamic rescue front, and another that supports the more moderate Algerian "Hamas" headed by Mahfoud Nahnah. In the late 1980s, especially after the Mujahidin victory in Afghanistan, the volunteers began returning to Algeria, taking with them rich battle experience in guerilla warfare and Islamic revolutionary fervor.

These volunteers, who upon their return were called "Afghans," were integrated into radical Islamic organizations such as the "Armed Islamic Movement" (GIA) and "Al Takfir-wal Hijrah" organization.[9]

Ali Belhaj, one of the leaders of the Islamic front in Algeria, was the spiritual father of most of the radical resistance organizations there, and some believe it was he who paved the way for the "Afghan groups" to be integrated into the organizational system of the Islamic Front, in order to institutionalize a radical militant power base that would work against the attempt of some movement leaders to move toward diplomatic compromise and political struggle.[10]

The first violent action of the "Afghans" took place in November 1991 in the village of Gomar on the Algerian-Tunisian border. A group of fighters attacked a police station, killing and wounding many.[11] Since November 1991, as the struggle between the regime in Algeria and the Islamic opposition has grown stronger, there have again been reports of the Afghans' involvement in terrorist activity throughout the country.

Terrorist activity by Islamic organizations which began in 1991 with sporadic attacks against military targets and government institutions gradually spread, becoming a civil war that has claimed 70,000 lives to date. During this period Islamic terrorist organizations have managed to seize control of many positions in rural areas and even of certain districts in large cities.

In 1994 Islamic terrorist elements took steps to broaden the front of their struggle and, after a short ultimatum, began to strike at foreign targets and citizens in Algeria. It should be noted that some 60,000 foreign workers live and work in Algeria, many of them in the oil industry which is the country's and the regime's main source of income.[12]

Since 1994, and especially during 1995-1996, the G.I.A. began to conduct terrorist attacks abroad. All of these attacks took place in France or against French citizens outside France and were explained as responding to the French government's support of the present government in Algeria. The worsening conflict between the G.I.A. and France was also explained by its spokesmen in the context of the historical dispute between Algeria and France during the Algerian civil war in the early 1960s.

The G.I.A.'s terror apparatus abroad included hijacking an Air France airplane in December 1994, and two waves of attacks in France (July-October 1995 and December 1996) which killed approximately twenty people and injured dozens.

As an Islamic terrorist organization, the G.I.A. — like other fundamentalist organizations in Arab countries — advocates the establishment of a religious Islamic regime, and sees the US, Israel and Judaism as the enemies of Islam. Despite this, the organization has not performed an act of terror directed specifically against American and Israeli targets. The G.I.A. has however, made attacks on Jewish targets in France as part of its larger terrorist campaign in that country. These attacks included two car bombs near a synagogue in Lyon on December 24 (that were defused) and near a Jewish school in Villeurbanne near Lyon (September 1995), and a letter bomb sent to the editor of a Jewish newspaper (December 1996).

As a result of the G.I.A. terror attacks abroad, all of which took place exclusively in France, its infrastructure which was scattered throughout various European countries — mainly France, Belgium, Britain, Germany, Italy, Sweden, and Spain — was exposed. In these countries terrorist cells with a limited number of members were active and connected with each other, and shared the various logistical, financial and operational roles assigned. The main purpose of the European network was to collect funds and weapons and smuggle them to their co-combatants in Algeria.[13] Preventive and enforcement actions taken by security forces in Europe, at French initiative and with international cooperation, damaged the infrastructure of the Algerian terrorist network and put a stop to G.I.A. terrorist activity in the international arena.

It should be stressed that until now, unlike Palestinian and Shiite terrorist organizations, the G.I.A. has not conducted "blackmail" operations to effect the release of the dozens of its members who are imprisoned in various countries in Europe. This policy may be the result of the organization's desire to focus its struggle in Algeria and avoid invoking the wrath of European public opinion in a way that would damage its ability to use Europe as an essential logistical base for its activity in Algeria.

It should also be noted that in 1998 more terrorist cells connected with the G.I.A. were discovered in Europe. The involvement of immigrants and the children of immigrants from the Maghreb countries in terrorist attacks in France, as well as in the Algerian terrorist cells in other European countries, indicates a broad infrastructure for recruiting potential volunteers for Islamic terrorist organizations. These volunteers come from immigrant populations with low socio-economic standing which suffer from a sense of neglect and social alienation in their country of residence. These populations served as sources for recruitment of new volunteers, some of whom were sent for terrorist training in Afghanistan in the early 1990s, and some who volunteered to fight in Bosnia.

Tunisia[14]

Tunisian intelligence claimed that in May 1992 Islamic extremists who were trained in Afghanistan tried to assassinate the President of Tunisia Ben Ali by shooting down his airplane with a shoulder-launched missile. The attempt failed and the would-be assassins were caught. To date the security forces in Tunisia are managing to successfully thwart Islamic extremists in their country, with the activities of these groups prohibited and most of their leaders banned or having fled, principally Rashid Ghannushi, who is the head of the "Al-Nahada" movement.

Nevertheless, the violent struggle between the regime and the Islamic opposition in neighboring Algeria, particularly if the extremist Islamic movement rises to power in Algeria, will no doubt have a far-reaching impact on affairs in Tunisia.

Yemen

Yemen is currently an important center for Afghan alumni activities and organizations because of the authorities' "tolerant" attitude toward them.

Yemen is a meeting place for activists and a relatively "safe" hub for their movement around the world.

In December 1998 the Yemenite authorities arrested a group of Islamic extremists who had planned attacks against British and American targets in Aden.[15]

The group, led by the Muslim cleric Abu Hamza who resides in London, was identified with a radical Islamic group called "Supporters of Shariah" and included eight Britons and two Algerians.

Members of the group came to Yemen on false French passports and received arms and training from the local fundamentalist Islamic organization "Islamic Army of Aden," headed by Ahmed Al Mihdar, who was executed after being convicted of kidnapping sixteen European tourists.[16]

During Al Mihdar's trial it was revealed that members of the Islamic Army that he headed had kidnapped the European tourists in order to bring about the release of members of their group who had been arrested in December 1998.[17]

The kidnapping came to an end with a rescue mission launched by the Yemenite security forces in which the kidnappers and four hostages were killed.

Examination of those involved in the two terrorist events in Yemen shows that some of them were trained in Afghanistan and had connections with the Egyptian Jihad which was supported by Bin Laden.

In October 2000 an attack was made on the American destroyer "Cole" which was anchored at Aden. A boat-bomb, piloted by a suicide attacker, exploded adjacent to the destroyer and caused deaths, injuries and heavy damage to the vessel. The incident is still under investigation as a result of limited cooperation from the Yemenite government, but it is already clear that Bin Laden was behind the attack.

Egypt

In the 1980s Egypt backed Muslim and Western countries in condemning the Soviet invasion of Afghanistan and providing aid to the Mujahidin who waged battle against the Kabul government and the Soviet forces. In this context Egypt permitted Egyptian volunteers to go to Afghanistan to participate in the Mujahidins' struggle. Most of these volunteers came from the ranks of the Muslim Brotherhood and more radical organizations such as the Egyptian Islamic Jihad.[18] The Egyptian authorities at that time welcomed the opportunity to send the "revolutionary fervor" of the radical Islamic elements out of the country, thus reducing radical activity at home and strengthening Egypt's standing in the Muslim community.

Over time, however, it seems that sending the volunteers to Afghanistan became a double-edged sword for the Egyptian regime. After the end of the struggle against the Soviets and the fall of the pro-Soviet regime in Kabul, the Egyptian volunteers began returning to Egypt. This time the Egyptian authorities worked to prevent their return out of fear that they would join

The Endless Jihad... 129

radical terrorist groups in Egypt. At least some however, found their way back to Egypt and joined Islamic terrorist organizations there. From 1992 to 1994, "Afghans" were involved in a long series of terrorist operations in Egypt. At the trials, which became known as the "Afghan returnee" trials, some of the activities of these elements in terrorist organizations working against the regime in Egypt were exposed.

Egyptian Mujahidin activities included:

- Establishing training camps in Afghanistan and in Peshawar in Pakistan.[19]
- Returning the fighters to Egypt after a training period, mainly through the Sudan.[20]
- Preparation of false documentation for these fighters.[21]
- Cultivation and trade in drugs in order to fund the organizations' activities.[22]
- Propaganda and publicity operations of the terrorist organizations – Tala al Fatah and Egyptian Islamic Jihad.[23]
- A center for planning and initiating attacks in Egypt and elsewhere – some of those involved in the attack on the Twin Towers in New York came from Afghanistan.[24]

Following are a number of examples of the terrorist activity in which these elements were involved in Egypt:

- From 1992-1993 extremist Islamic activists who were involved in violent activity in upper Egypt were arrested and tried.
  During their interrogation they confessed that they had been trained in Afghanistan and their intention had been to launch terrorist attacks against security forces and public figures in Egypt.[25]
- During this time there were attempts to assassinate the Egyptian Minister of Propaganda Sawfat El Sharif[26] and the Egyptian premier Atef Sidky. The assassins who were captured were members of the Tala al Fatah that was established in Afghanistan.[27]

The Egyptian terrorist organizations marked tourists in their country as a preferred target with the clear intention of causing double injury to the regime: by damaging the economy (tourism is the second most important source of income, after income from the Suez Canal), and by damaging the regime's prestige and image in both the internal and international arenas. The exhibitionist terrorist attacks carried out against tourists were meant to instill a sense of insecurity at home concerning the regime's stability, and to encourage recruitment on the international front of new volunteers to Egyptian organizations.

The tourism seasons in Egypt in 1992-1993 were severely damaged and the direct injury to the country's treasury was in the billions of dollars. The worst attack on tourists was carried out by the Al Gama'ah al Islamiyyah against tourists at the Hatshepsut temple in Luxor (November 1997), where fifty-eight tourists and four Egyptians were killed. The attack inflicted serious damage on Egypt's recovering tourist industry and caused physical damage estimated at another half a billion dollars.

The strike against tourism also served the ideological goal of injuring foreigners who represent Western culture which "denies and sullies" the Muslim world.

The Coptic minority was also a target for attacks because it is perceived by Egyptian fundamentalist organizations as a religious, cultural and ethnic foreign seed, and because extremist Islamic elements were jealous of their economic success.

In November 1993 President Rabbani of Afghanistan visited Egypt and signed a cooperation and extradition agreement. Egypt offered Afghanistan economic and security aid in exchange for Afghanistan not harboring Egyptian Islamic extremists and its extradition of senior activists such as Mohammed Shauqi al Islambuli.[28]

At the end of his visit President Rabbani expressed his appreciation of Egypt's contribution to the victory of the Mujahidin in Afghanistan, condemned all forms of terror and declared that he would not allow Afghan territory to be used as a staging area for threatening the stability of the Egyptian government.[29]

Rabbani's desire to improve his country's relations with Egypt were different from his rival Hekmatyar's, who offered patronage to Egyptian fundamentalism in Afghanistan and even offered political asylum to Sheikh Omar Abd el Rahman (following the request that Egypt extradite him to the US after his involvement in the Twin Towers attack became known).

Because Rabbani's government was unable to enforce its authority on the opposition movements led by Hekmatyar,[30] Egypt announced at the time that it would not act to actualize the agreements so long as Afghanistan did not fulfil its obligations to deport or extradite fundamentalist Egyptian terrorists found in its territory.[31]

Later, with most of the territory of Afghanistan held by the Taliban, which the Egyptian government has not acknowledged, it seems that the agreement has lost all practical significance.

The security forces' hard-line approach against terrorist organizations in Egypt and the deportation of activists curtailed these organizations' freedom of movement and also forced them to conduct terrorist attacks outside their country. Most of the attacks were carried out as revenge for arrests, extraditions and assassinations of their people abroad by Egyptian security forces, often in cooperation with local security forces. The Egyptian Jihad thus assassinated an Egyptian diplomat in Switzerland (November 1995), the Al Gama'ah al Islamiyyah exploded a car bomb driven by a suicide bomber in a police station in Rieka, Croatia (October 1995), and the Egyptian embassy in Pakistan was blown up (November 1995). The most prominent attempted attack outside the borders of Egypt was the Al Gama'ah al Islamiyyah's attempted assassination of President Mubarak during his visit to Ethiopia (June 1995). The perpetrators hoped to harm the president outside the tight security circle that protects him inside Egypt.

Egyptian organizations, mainly the Al Gama'ah al Islamiyyah, have been involved in international terror by means of Egyptian citizens, "Afghan alumni" (those trained in Mujahidin camps after the end of the war), who worked alone in independent Islamic terrorist cells abroad.

It must be noted that the blind Egyptian sheikh, Omar Abd El Rahman, who is the highest spiritual authority of the Al Gama'ah al Islamiyyah and the Egyptian Jihad, is responsible for giving religious sanction to these terrorist cells.

The Egyptian organizations' activity in recent years, especially since 1998, has been influenced by their ties with Osama Bin Laden and Al Qaeda. Al Qaeda absorbed a significant number of Egyptians into its ranks. At least one of the suicide drivers who drove the car bombs in Nairobi and Dar Es Salaam in August 1998 for Al Qaeda was an Egyptian citizen. The alliance between Bin Laden and the Egyptian organizations is reflected in his close ties with the heads of Egyptian organizations such as Ahmed Rifa'i Taha, head of the diplomatic council and Mustafa Hamza, head of the military wing of the Al Gama'ah al Islamiyyah and especially Ayman Zawahiri, head of one of the Egyptian Jihad factions. The closest tie is with Ayman Zawahiri, who subordinated his attack policy to Bin Laden's strategy of action. According to this strategy, terror activity must be redirected from attacks on Egyptian targets to attacking American ones. The frontal confrontation with the Egyptian regime causes the deaths of innocent people in Egypt and alienation of the Egyptian Muslim population, in contrast to the support that attacks on the American infidels are likely to arouse among Muslims. The adoption of this operational strategy by the Egyptian Jihad was reflected in the attack it planned against the US embassy in Albania which was thwarted in June 1998, and also in its people's involvement in the attacks in east Africa in August 1998.

Al Gama'ah al Islamiyyah, which according to Bin Laden's understanding was supposed to be the central framework in a religious military coalition that he formed, has in the last two years been hesitant about his policy with regard to the struggle against the Egyptian regime and the US.

The declaration issued by its leaders, who are jailed in Egypt, of a cease-fire with the Egyptian regime (July 1997) engendered an argument between its leadership in Egypt and abroad with regard to its policy on attacks and locations. The massacre of tourists at Luxor (Oct. 1997) aggravated this dispute mainly because of pressure put on organization members in Egypt and abroad by the Egyptian regime.

The blind sheikh's declaration from his prison in the US from which it could be understood that the organization should strive to attain its objectives in peaceful ways (October 1998), tipped the scales in favor of those supporting an end to violent terror in Egypt.

The Al Gama'ah al Islamiyyah has already formally announced a "cease-fire" and, after the resignation of Ayman Zawahiri, part of the Egyptian Jihad organization also declared a unilateral "cease-fire." This declaration also gave rise to disagreement in the Egyptian movement and the question of fulfilling it still has not been settled.

"Jordanian Afghans"

At the beginning of 1994 there were a series of explosions in cinemas in Jordan.[32] In 1995, following arrests made by the Jordanian security services, cooperation between the group "Bai'at al Imam" (Pledge of Allegiance to Imam) – headed by Issam Mohammed al Burqawi, known as Abu Mohammed Al Muqadassi, a Palestinian hailing from Jaffa – and a number of "Afghan alumni" was revealed.[33]

The goal of this collaboration was to banish what they regarded as the corrupt regime from Jordan by means of Jihad, as part of the comprehensive struggle to repair Islamic society. Weapons and explosives were found in the possession of the group's members.

It emerged from their interrogation that they had intended to carry out extensive terrorist activity against elements they regarded as identified with the government's corruption, including public figures, cinemas and hotels.

In December 1999 an Islamic terrorist collaboration was exposed in Jordan that included Jordanian citizens, an Iraqi, an Algerian and Palestinians with American papers.

The group was led by Abu Hushar, who had already been arrested in Jordan (1993) on charges of attacks against the kingdom but was pardoned by the king and released. Abu Hushar himself was trained in Afghanistan, returned to Jordan and established "Mohammed's Army" which was also partly comprised of Afghan alumni.[34]

On December 17, 1999 Halil Dik, who is considered responsible for the collaboration and planning of attacks in Jordan that were thwarted, was extradited from Pakistan to Jordan.

Interrogation of the collaborating members showed that they had intended to carry out attacks against Jewish and Israeli tourists at the Radisson hotel in Amman, visitors to Moses' tomb at Mount Nebo, the border crossings between Jordan and Israel, and pilgrims visiting Jesus' baptism site.[35]

Actions Against Jewish and Israeli Targets Abroad

Despite the venomous rhetoric of the Afghan alumni and Bin Laden, whose style recalls the "Protocols of the Elders of Zion," until now it has not resulted in waves of terror against Jewish and Israeli targets in the international arena. Nevertheless, in the latter half of the 1990s these organizations carried out a number of attacks and attempted attacks against Israeli and Jewish targets abroad. The first took place in New York in November 1990 when a fundamentalist Muslim murdered Rabbi Meir Kahana. In June 1993 an Islamic terror network's plan to carry out a series of attacks in New York, including the UN building, FBI headquarters and the assassination of a Jewish American senator, was foiled. This terror network operated with the approval and religious inspiration of the blind Egyptian sheikh Omar Abd el Rahman. It transpired that Sayyid Nutzair, Kahana's murderer was connected with the Egyptian sheikh and the terror network involved in the thwarted attacks in June 1993.

In Egypt, the Al Gama'ah al Islamiyyah perpetrated an attack on tourists at the Europa hotel in Cairo (during Operation Grapes of Wrath in Lebanon), killing 17 Greek pilgrims. In the announcement in which they claimed responsibility, the organization stated that the attack was originally aimed at Israeli tourists who usually use that hotel.

According to the testimony of a senior activist who stood trial in Egypt in April 1999 in the "Albanian returnees" affair, the Egyptian Jihad under the leadership of Dr. Ayman Zawahiri, which is part of Bin Laden's terror network, planned to carry out attacks against Israeli targets throughout the world.[36]

The Algerian G.I.A. carried out three attacks against Jewish targets in France as part of their comprehensive terror campaign in that country in the latter half of the 1990s. These included placing two car bombs, one near a synagogue in Lyon in 1994 (which was defused) and one next to a Jewish school in Villeurbanne near Lyon (1995). In the last attack the bomb exploded and only because of a malfunction that caused the school bell announcing the end of the day to ring a few minutes late, was a mass killing of the Jewish school children avoided. A letter bomb also suspected to have been sent by Islamic fundamentalists was received by the editor of a Jewish newspaper in France (1996).

In 1995 several members of the Bai'at al Imam group (Pledge of Allegiance to Imam) – which was led by Issam Mohammed al Burqawi (known as Abu Mohammed Al Muqadassi), a Palestinian from Jaffa – including several Afghan Mujahidin, were arrested in Jordan.

Members of the cell had planned attacks on Israeli targets in Jordan. And, in July 1997, members of a group that had planned to infiltrate into Israel to carry out attacks were arrested.[37]

One can assume that the relative infrequency of attacks / attempted attacks thus far by Afghan alumni on Israeli and Jewish targets abroad is the result of:

1. Focusing their struggle first and foremost against anti-Islamic regimes in their countries of origin with a view to replacing them with Islamic regimes that follow Shariah.
2. Their "making do" with sporadic attacks only against these targets within the their composite terror activities against non-Muslim adversaries.
3. Focusing terror activity on American targets, given that America is perceived as the primary and central adversary which must be attacked in defense of Islam.

Intensification of Activity Against Israel

In the year 2000 the possibility has arisen that Afghan alumni under Bin Laden's leadership have decided to focus part of their activities on Israeli targets abroad and even inside Israel.

The event that demonstrates this trend more than any other is the terror system that was uncovered in Jordan in December 1999 with the arrest of a fundamentalist Islamic terror network. This affair marked a watershed in the activity against Israel directed by central activists in Al Qaeda.

The Jordanian terror network included Jordanian citizens, an Iraqi and an Algerian, and Palestinians with American documentation.

In their interrogation the detainees confessed to having been trained in Afghanistan at a training camp funded by Bin Laden and assisted by contact people from Al Qaeda in Pakistan and Afghanistan.[38] Several members of the network were trained in Lebanon with the aid of the Hizbullah and Palestinian opponents of Arafat.

Network members planned to carry out fatal attacks on Jewish and American tourists at the Radisson hotel in Amman, Israeli visitors to Moses' tomb on

Mount Nebo, and Israelis and Jordanians at border crossings between the two countries. They also intended to kill pilgrims visiting Jesus' baptismal site.[39]

One of the prominent characteristics of this affair was the central role of Palestinian Afghan alumni among the members of the network and its collaborators outside Jordan. The central activists who were responsible for logistical aid and granting religious sanction for the attacks were Zain El Abdin, known as Abu Zbayda, a Palestinian from Gaza; Amar Abu Amar, known as Abu Katada, a Palestinian; and Hussein Halil Dik, a Palestinian with an American passport who worked from Afghanistan, Pakistan and Britain.

A new phenomenon worthy of attention is the effort Bin Laden's people are making to recruit Palestinian activists resident in the occupied territories for operations inside Israel. Although this is not yet, as far as we know, a sweeping phenomenon, a number of arrests made in the past years make it imperative to prepare for such an eventuality.

In February 2000, for example, Hindawi, a Palestinian whose family came from Halhul and an Afghan alumnus who lived in Lebanon for many years, was arrested. His family had returned to Israel with the establishment of the Palestinian Authority. The detainee's father is the Authority's chief of police in Hebron. During interrogation Hindawi admitted that in 1998 he trained in guerrilla warfare and terror at the Durante camp, which is one of Osama Bin Laden's main training centers in Afghanistan. Sketches for the assembly of explosive devices were found in his possession. Despite his denial, he is suspected of planning to carry out attacks in Israel, in all likelihood with the cooperation of local Palestinians.[40]

On August 21, 2000 the arrest in June of a terrorist network was made public. Nabil Okal, a Palestinian from the Jabaliya refugee camp in Gaza who was head of the network, was trained in marksmanship and explosives during 1997 at a camp belonging to Osama Bin Laden in Afghanistan. When he returned to the territories he recruited a number of activists from the West Bank and Gaza and Israeli Arab members of the Islamic movements. He intended to dispatch them for training in Afghanistan. Okal admitted that he was in contact with Sheikh Yassin, the spiritual leader of Hamas, had revealed to him that he was trained in Afghanistan and had received money from him to fund the organization. The network intended to carry out widespread attacks inside Israel, including suicide attacks, kidnapping of soldiers and even missile attacks on settlements.[41]

It is unclear what motivated Bin Laden and the Afghan alumni he supports to intensify terrorist activity against Israeli targets, and moreover, to act inside the State of Israel. However, the main reason may be the criticism voiced against Bin Laden for focusing only on American targets and neglecting the struggle to liberate the holy sites in Palestine, together with the increasing involvement of Palestinians in the Islamic front.

Azerbaijan[42]

After the defeat suffered by the Azar forces (Muslims) in the war with the Armenians (Christians) for control of the Nogorno Karabach region, Azerbaijan approached Afghanistan in August 1993 with a request for military assistance. Afghanistan acceded to the request and dispatched around a thousand Mujahidin fighters to help the Azars in combat. In October 1993 the Afghan Mujahidin launched a surprise attack against the Armenian forces in the Zanglan region (near the Iranian border) and went so far as to make ground advancements until they were once again rebuffed by an Armenian counter-attack. A part of these Mujahidin forces, as far as we know, have remained in Azerbaijan and continue to assist that country in its struggle against the Armenians.

Chechnya[43]

Subsequent to the dismantling of the USSR, a religious nationalist awakening took palace in Chechnya which led the leaders of the separatist stream to declare their secession from the USSR on September 6, 1991 and to establish the Chechnyan Republic of Ichkeria.

Russia, under President Yeltsin, was not amenable to the Chechnyan separatist move and tried, through aid to power centers within Chechnya and direct Russian involvement, to effect a change of regime in the country.

The failure of the Russian move created a situation of *de facto* independence in Chechnya and accelerating tension between the countries.

The tension continued and finally culminated on December 11, 1994, with the Russian invasion of Chechnya.

Since that time, the Russians and the Chechnyans have been engaged in a conflict that ranges from regular and semi-regular forces to guerilla warfare and terror employed by the Chechnyans.

The Mujahidin regime after the victory in 1992 and the Taliban regime has provided equipment, arms and combatants to the Chechnyan Islamic separatists in their struggle against Russia.

Other Islamic elements that provide aid to Chechnya derive from the Wahabbi movement in Saudi Arabia and even Bin Laden's organization.

Afghan alumni volunteers are active in the Chechnyan ranks. They are headed by Ibn Al Qutb, who garnered rich battle command experience in Afghanistan and Tajikistan before joining the fray in Chechnya.

The Afghans shared with the Chechnyans their extensive experience in guerilla warfare and terror, as well as their familiarity with the doctrine of war and the weak points of the Russians whom they had taken on in Afghanistan and Tajikistan.

Bosnia

In 1993 it became known that some 300 "Arabic Afghan" Mujahidin from Algeria, Sudan and Saudi Arabia were active in central and northern Bosnia.

These Mujahidin took active part in fighting against the Serbian forces while also engaging in educating and recruiting the Bosnian population toward adopting their fundamentalist world view. A Mujahidin member related in an interview that his movement had two goals in Bosnia: Jihad against the Serbs and action (Dawa) towards educating the Bosnian Muslims to "true Islam."[44] In the wake of the war in Kosovo, "Afghan alumni" began operating in this region as well, and it appears that there is similar involvement in the conflict between Muslims and the regime in Macedonia.

Independent Terror Cells

One of the most prominent characteristics of international terror in recent years has been the activity of autonomous split "Islamic terrorist cells" with no defined structural hierarchy. These cells operate through mutual connections and ties with other institutionalized terror organizations. The Afghan alumni play a central role in their operations, utilizing the skills acquired in their training in Afghanistan and their contacts with Islamic NGOs which provide logistical support and fund their activity. The terror cells have been responsible, among other things, for the February 1993 attack on the Twin Towers in New York that killed six and injured approximately a thousand people, for planning the thwarted attacks on the UN building and the main tunnels connecting New York and New Jersey (June 1993), for an attack on a Philippine Airlines flight (December 1994), and for the planning of a terror scheme against American airplanes in Asia that was meant to take place in early 1995.

Investigation of these terror cells led to the exposure of their ties with Islamic non-government organizations such as the IWL (Islamic World League), IIRO

(Islamic International Relief Organization) and Islamic cultural centers in Europe such as the one in Milan. Extensive links between their members and Osama Bin Laden's organization were also revealed.

Osama Bin Laden

One of the prominent products of the Jihad in Afghanistan is Osama Bin Laden. Osama Bin Laden is one of the fifty three children of Mohammed Awad Bin Laden – a wealthy Saudi businessman of Yemenite extraction. Bin Laden Senior is the owner of one of the largest construction companies in the Middle East (Bin Laden Co.), and his fortune is estimated at US $5 billion.[45]

Osama Bin laden was born in 1957,[46] and he is a graduate of the King Abed El Aziz University in Jedda (Saudi Arabia) having studied civil engineering. He joined the family business, and his personal fortune at the time was estimated at US $300 million.

After the Soviet Union's invasion of Afghanistan and the Afghan Mujahidins' call to their brothers in the Muslim world to launch a Jihad, Osama Bin Laden left Saudi Arabia and together with groups of supporters and heavy engineering equipment, came to Pakistan and joined in the Afghan Mujahidin's struggle. Initially Bin Laden dealt with establishing an apparatus for recruiting Arab volunteers for the Jihad: he funded their recruitment and travel to Pakistan, where they were trained to fight against the Soviets in a camp that he had established.

During this period close working relations were formed bewteen Bin Laden and the Palestinian Abdullah Azam, who was one of the Jihad's spiritual fathers in Afghanistan.

From 1986 onward Bin Laden no longer contented himself with the organization and training of volunteers, and himself joined in the fighting in Afghanistan at the head of a group of volunteers which he led in a series of battles against Soviet forces.

At the end of the 1980s Bin Laden returned to Saudi Arabia and was received as a hero in radical Islamic circles. Very soon he began inciting against the Saudi regime, which he perceived as corrupt and heretical. Bin Laden's relations with the Saudi government reached crisis point when he openly criticized Saudia's agreement to deployment of United States and coalition forces on its territory during the Gulf War.

Against this background Bin Laden fled from Saudi Arabia to Sudan, together with a group of "Afghan Alumni," and continued to manage his affairs and his subversive activities from there. In 1994 the Saudi government revoked his citizenship and put a price on his head.

Bin Laden established an economic empire in the Sudan which included leatherwork factories, construction companies, a bank, agricultural farms and import-export companies. The extensive economic system provided employment for his "Afghan Alumni" friends and sources of income to fund his subversive activities. The latter included the establishment and management of training camps for Islamic terrorists from the world over.

From his station in the Sudan Bin Laden began to outline his international terror network, with his operatives actively participating in various conflicts: Somalia, Bosnia, Kosovo, Chechniya, etc.

Bin Laden was closely allied with the Sudanese leaders Omar Al Bashir and Hasan Al Turabi, and resided in Khartoum in a compound well guarded by Sudanese security forces. During his stay in the Sudan Bin Laden survived an attempted assassination. Following heavy pressure placed on the Sudan by the United States and Saudi Arabia, Bin Laden was forced to leave the Sudan and move to Afghanistan in May of 1996.

Upon returning to Afghanistan, which was still under the Mujahidin regime headed by Rabbani and Masoud in Kabul, Bin Laden settled in the city of Jalalabad which was held by the Taliban at the time. Only months after his return the Taliban conquered Kabul and most of Afghanistan, and Bin Laden enjoyed freedom of movement throughout the country.

In February 1997 the Taliban rejected an American proposal offering international recognition of their regime in exchange for the extradition of Bin Laden. In March 1997 Bin Laden survived another assassination attempt which involved the explosion of two bombs that left fifty killed and one hundred and fifty wounded. Bin Laden himself was not hurt.

Following the assassination attempt Bin Laden moved to the city of Kandahar – the Taliban movement's hub of power. The Taliban's official claim was that Bin Laden had moved to Kandahar so that they could keep an eye on his movements and activities and prevent him from being involved in any terrorist activities . Several journalists even reported that Bin Laden was under house arrest although these reports were never verified.

Nonetheless, Bin Laden continued to operate training camps in Afghanistan, where hundreds of Islamic terror activists were trained and then sent to set up terror cells of the Al Qaeda organization around the world.

Al Qaeda

Another key organization in the activities of the Afghan alumni, whose influence has been felt in the international arena in recent years in particular, is Al Qaeda. This organization was established in 1988 by Saudi millionaire Osama Bin Laden.

Al Qaeda was established in the services office (Maktab al-Khidamat) as an Islamic non-governmental organization handling the recruitment, absorption and dispatch of thousands of Islamic volunteers from 50 countries throughout the world to the Mujahidin camps in Afghanistan and Pakistan.

After the war most activity was conducted from the Sudan and Afghanistan by means of a worldwide network of offices, including in the US (especially at the Al Kafach center in Brooklyn) and the Philippines.

Al Qaeda provided aid to other terrorist organizations and maintains links with them, working to radicalize Islamic movements active in Chechnya, Bosnia, Tajikistan, Somalia, Kashmir, Yemen, and Kosovo. Alongside this support its members were involved in carrying out terrorist attacks. Al Qaeda was accused of direct involvement in the attack on UN forces in Somalia in October 1993 in which 18 American soldiers were killed, and in the attacks in Kenya and Tanzania in August 1998. There is also evidence of a clear connection between Al Qaeda and terrorist attacks that were planned and executed by terror cells led by Ramsi Yusuf in New York (1993) and the Philippines (1994), and of involvement in the attack on an America target in Riyadh in which six people were killed, five of them American soldiers (November 1995). The Saudis claimed that Bin Laden had no connection with the latter two incidents, but it is likely that their perpetrators were influenced by his preaching about struggle against American imperialism.

Intensification of the Conflict between Bin Laden and the US

In 1998 the question of the Afghan alumni once again reached the international agenda, mainly because of the showcase attacks carried out in east Africa by Al Qaeda. Bin Laden was accused by the US of being the mastermind behind these attacks, and was presented in the Western and Arab media as the embodiment of the fundamentalist threat of terror in the international arena. Bin Laden contributed to this by presuming to lead what he called "the religious-cultural-historical struggle between Islam and the Jewish-Crusader alliance" which aims to vanquish Islam and conquer its sacred territories.[47]

In a series of interviews and publications, such as "The Declaration of War of

June 1996"[48] and the *fatwa* he published in February 1998, Bin Laden presented a world view that claims that the entire world and the Middle East in particular are the site of a deterministic struggle for survival between the three great religions. In this struggle a Christian ("Crusader" in his term)«Jewish coalition has taken shape, embodied in the US and Israel (and world Jewry), in order to conquer Islam's most sacred territories, Mecca, Medina and Jerusalem, and seeking to vanquish Islam. According to him this alliance is performing a systematic, intentional massacre of Muslims. By way of example he offered the massacre of the Iraqi Muslim population by the American forces during the Gulf war in 1991, the bombing of Iraq in December 1998, the massacre at Sabra and Shatila in Lebanon, and the killing of Palestinians by Israel in the occupied territories, etc.[49]

In order to enlist and motivate the population of believers Bin Laden needed concepts with historical significance and an Islamic context such as "Crusaders" and "Jihad." He justified the violence that he advocated in terms of defense of the sanctity of Islam, and he presented Muslims as the victims.

According to him the use of violence and terror were meant to prove to his followers that the enemies of Islam, even those that appeared invincible like the US and USSR, are vulnerable because of the weakness of their beliefs. Bin Laden leans to a large extent on the ethos of the successful struggle in Afghanistan, which in his view led to the dismantling of the Soviet empire. Bin Laden presented other examples of the enemy's weakness, such as the retreat of American forces from Somalia which he claimed had been effected by guerilla activities that he supported. The attacks carried out by opposition forces in Riyadh (November 1995) and Dahran (June 1996) which caused the deaths of twenty-four and wounded dozens of Americans were part of the struggle, with the dual goals of "purification" of the holy sites in Mecca and Medina, which were under American occupation, and moral-psychological victory of the warriors of Islam. Bin Laden predicted a similar fate for Israel, which occupies the holy ground of Al Aksa.[50]

During 1998 Bin Laden gathered an Islamic coalition around him that was meant to help him consolidate a front in opposition to the Jewish-Crusader alliance.

On February 23, 1998, he convened the heads of a number of Islamic organizations in Afghanistan and declared the establishment of the "International Islamic Front for Jihad against the Crusaders and Jews" (hereinafter the "Front"). The "Front" published a religious dictum signed by the leaders of four Islamic organizations including: Osama Bin Laden, head of Al Qaeda; Ayman Al Zawahiri, head of a faction of the Egyptian Islamic Jihad; Ahmed Rifai Te, head of the Egyptian Al Gama'ah al Islamiyyah; Sheikh Mir Hamza, secretary of the

Pakistani Jamiat el Ulama; and Fazlul Rhaman, the emir of the Jihad movement in Bangladesh. Because Bin Laden has no religious training or authority and did not have significant military-terrorist forces at his disposal, he needed the backup and support of these organization leaders. Religious figures, especially Sheikh Mir Hamza, who was considered an Islamic spiritual authority, gave religious-legal validity to the decisions of the Islamic Front while the leaders of the Al Gama'ah al Islamiyyah and the Egyptian Jihad gave the Front its military-terrorist backbone.

In a Fatwa published by the Front its leaders called on all Muslims in the world to see it as their personal obligation to kill Americans and their allies, both civilians and military personnel, in order to liberate the holy mosque in Mecca (i.e., Saudi Arabia) from their occupation and Al Aqsa (i.e., Jerusalem in particular and Palestine in general).[51]

In May 1998 Bin Laden granted an interview to ABC in which he declared before the American viewing public the Front's intention to carry out attacks against civilians in the world because of the "criminal policy" of the American government. Tripartite cooperation between the US, Egypt and Albania led to an attack planned by members of the Egyptian Jihad/Zawahiri faction against the US embassy in Tirana being thwarted, and their extradition to Egypt (July 1998). After this activity the Front and the Egyptian Jihad sent overt threats of attacks on American targets to the *Al Hayat* newspaper[52]. The following day, August 7, members of Al Qaeda were responsible for two showcase attacks in Kenya and Tanzania against US embassies, which resulted in 291 dead and some 5000 wounded, most of them local civilians. Of the American citizens who were the primary target of the attack, twelve employees of the US embassy in Nairobi were killed.

The attacks in east Africa "granted" the US a pretext for a military-force action against the threat posed to it in recent years by the Afghan alumni under Bin Laden and the Egyptian organizations. The unequivocal proof obtained in the interrogation of detainees who had participated in the planning and execution of the attacks was made public and served as justification for the bombing of Al Qaeda bases in Afghanistan and the Sudan and the concomitant damage to the sovereignty of the countries that harbored the organization. The American bombing (August 20, 1998) was directed at five Al Qaeda camps in Afghanistan and a drug factory in Khartoum which, according to the US, was funded by Bin Laden and manufactured chemical weapons for him.

Along with military and intelligence activity, the US and Britain also worked against the Taliban on the diplomatic front. In this context the US dispatched ambassador Richardson to Afghanistan in an attempt to convince the Taliban to extradite Bin Laden for arrest, or to rein in his actions and statements against it.

142, for its part, offered the Taliban a deal by which it would agree to their opening a communications office in London and would restrict the activity of the leader of the opposition movement who lived in London in exchange for their restricting Bin Laden's activities.[53]

As yet, despite promises from senior Taliban officials to restrain him, the Taliban have not responded to the demand to extradite Bin Laden to the US or prevent him from threatening the execution of acts of terror against it. Interviews given by Bin Laden to Arab and Western media at the end of 1998, in which he threatened to intensify the struggle against the US and its allies, attest to the limited efficacy of diplomatic actions in this respect.

The US continued at the same time to work with its Arab and European partners to thwart and arrest members of Al Qaeda and the Egyptian organizations. In September 1998 a number of key figures in Bin Laden's terror network were arrested.

Wahdi al Haj – a Christian from Lebanon who converted to Islam and until 1994 was Bin Laden's personal secretary in the Sudan, and until 1997 played a central role in establishing the infrastructure in Kenya which prepared the attacks carried out in east Africa in August 1998 – was arrested in Texas. El Haj had moved to Texas in 1997, in all likelihood to establish a terrorist infrastructure in the US.

On September 16 Mamduh Mohammed Mahmud Salim was arrested in Munich. Salim was one of Bin Laden's senior assistants, serving as financial and logistical assistant and supervisor of weaponry (perhaps even non-conventional weaponry). Salim was extradited from Germany to the US on December 24, 1998 and stood trial for his part in Bin Laden's terror network.

A number of members of Bin Laden's network were arrested in London, first Khaled Fuaz, Bin Laden's representative in London, a Saudi oppositionist and head of the "Advice and Reform" organization. The US demanded his extradition from Britain.

At the same time, in the second half of 1998 Egypt intensified its war on terror against activists of the Egyptian organizations abroad. In this context Egypt, with American mediation, gained the cooperation of a number of countries, such as Albania, Azerbaijan, Bulgaria, South Africa, Ecuador, Saudi Arabia, Kuwait, and the United Arab Emirates, for the extradition of terrorist members of the Egyptian Jihad and Bin Laden's network into its hands (this was called "the Albanian returnees affair"). This activity posed a difficult challenge for Bin Laden and his partners, and threatened the survival of the Islamic coalition.

The American bombing of Iraq on December 17-20, 1998, provided yet another pretext for Bin Laden to threaten harm to American citizens because of their support for the massacre that the US was perpetrating on the Iraqi Muslim population.

In a series of aggressive interviews for *Time*, *Newsweek* and the BBC, Bin Laden called on his Muslim brothers to renew their aggression against the foes of Islam.[54]

Osama Bin Laden's capacity to respond with attacks has not diminished despite the blows he has taken in recent months. He selects a mode of response depending upon the continued development of the conflict between Al Qaeda and the US. He might make an attempt to expand it and involve terror organizations that are connected with him as well as the Egyptian organizations, for example, the Indian organization (Harakat Al Ansar), the Philippine organization (Abu Sayyaf) and others.

In his interviews Bin Laden also related to his efforts to secure non-conventional weapons. He presents the attainment of such arms as a religious obligation, contending that every Muslim who prevents it is sinning against his faith. Bin Laden was intentionally obscure with regard to whether he possesses such weapons, and under what circumstances he would use it if and when it is acquired.[55]

His efforts to secure and manufacture non-conventional weaponry were the reason for close monitoring by the US even before he openly declared his plans in that respect. The American bombing of a drug factory in Khartoum was justified by, among other things, the claim that it was engaged in producing chemical weapons for Bin Laden. Even the extradition of Mamduh Salim, Bin Laden's purchasing and logistics assistant, from Germany to the US (December 24) was related to the acquisition of non-conventional materials.

On October 5, 1999, members of the Taliban's Olympic organization protested the International Olympic Committee's decision to ban Afghan athletes from participating in the Olympic games unless they did so as individuals.

The Taliban Sports Authority accused the US of applying pressure to the Olympic committee to prevent Afghan athletes from participating because the Taliban were not prepared to extradite Bin Laden. The IOC announced at the beginning of October that they no longer recognized the Afghan Olympic committee.

In March 2000, police detectives stormed a house in Auckland (New Zealand) and arrested four Afghan refugees who had been granted New Zealand citizenship. Maps and sketches of the atomic reactor south of Sydney in Australia were found in the house. Investigation of the incident revealed that the four were members of Bin Laden's terrorist organization and maintained ties with other Islamic terror organizations.

The suspicion is that the organization intended to carry out an attack on the atomic reactor near Sydney during the Olympic games. Information about the arrests and materials that emerged during the interrogation were conveyed to Australian security officials.[56] It may be that the planned attack was Bin Laden's response to the banning of the Afghan delegation of athletes.

Taliban leader Mullah Mohammed Omar made it clear that his country would not extradite Bin Laden since the Americans had not provided decisive proof of his involvement in terror attacks. "Since this is a Muslim who is a guest in our country and according to local custom a guest cannot be evicted, let alone extradited to an enemy," says Omar, "so even if half of Afghanistan is destroyed we will not extradite him."

The sanctions that the UN placed on Afghanistan in October 1999 came into effect automatically in November. The sanctions included two main restrictions: preventing international flights to and from Afghanistan, and freezing Taliban assets in banks around the world.

Since the Taliban hold very few assets in banks globally this sanction was not very significant. The flight sanction was serious because Afghanistan had been dependent on supplies for its health services, such as drugs that came in via the national carrier "Ariana." This was true also of food and other supplies that were imported by air. However, much of Afghanistan's "affairs" traditionally are performed through smuggling, which makes these sanctions not particularly effective and their significance largely declaratory. The deadly terrorist attacks on the Twin Towers and the Pentagon which caused thousands of deaths in the US, of which Bin Laden, hiding in Afghanistan, is accused, denotes a new era in the conflict between radical Islam, represented by the Taliban and Bin Laden, and the US and Western culture.

The US no longer sees or defines what happened as a terror attack but as a declaration of war and responded by declaring war on terrorism and its sponsors, such as the Taliban regime.
As these lines are written, the US and its coalition has destroyed the Taliban regime and the manhunt for Bin Laden is still underway.

Conclusion

In recent years, the phenomenon of the Afghan alumni has constituted a highly significant factor in the influence of international terror and its threat to the stability of regimes in Muslim countries.

This is a phenomenon that deviates from the narrow context of a terrorist organization or state-supported terror, and reflects a militant ideological religious stream that strives for change, cultural revolution and reinstating the glory of Islam.

The Afghan phenomenon can therefore be seen as an overt expression of cultural conflict in terms of Huntington's theory.

The Afghanistan war generated a number of extraordinary processes and phenomena in modern history, the most prominent of which are:

- The enlistment of volunteers from all over the Muslim world to help the Afghan Mujahidin in their struggle created for the first time a kind of **"international"** Islam.
- The experience and consolidation of these volunteer fighters led to contacts and connections among a variety of radical Islamic movements from all over the Muslim world.
- In the eyes of their supporters, the victory of these Islamic elements made them a glorious source of inspiration and hope for radical Islamic parties throughout the Muslim world.
- At the end of the war a large cadre of highly motivated fighters with rich operational experience took shape in Afghanistan. These people see the continued export of the Islamic revolution as their vocation. Osama Bin Laden is one of the prominent "outcomes" of the war in Afghanistan and his organization, Al Qaeda, is a key expression of the perception that reflects the "Afghan" phenomenon.

In his ideas, Osama Bin Laden unequivocally and bluntly expresses his vision of the struggle as a cultural conflict between Islam and other cultures, especially what he refers to as the "Christian – Jewish – Crusader" culture.

As manifestations of this cultural struggle, the actions of the Afghans are global. Their fight is taking place inside Muslim countries to change regimes and institute Islamic rule, on the lines of friction and conflict between Muslim minorities and governments (such as in the Balkans, the Caucasus, Kashmir, etc.), and in the international terror arena in a battle aimed primarily at the US, perceived as the source of evil in the world and the embodiment of Western culture – which from the fundamentalist perspective, constitutes today's main threat to Islam.

It appears that in coming years we will witness the continuation of the cultural conflict of which Huntington and Bin Laden, each from their own perspective and for their own reasons, both speak.

Epilogue

Following the terror attack on September 11, 2001 the United States demanded the immediate extradition of Osama Bin Laden, accused as being the mastermind of the attack, from Afghanistan. The Taliban government's refusal to extradite Bin Laden resulted in the USA declaring war on Bin Laden and the Taliban regime, which continued to offer him its patronage. In preparation for the battle in Afghanistan the USA established a broad coalition which included many Muslim countries, among them Pakistan, the former patron of the Taliban movement.

The coalition was intended to provide the USA with the international legitimization for military action in Afghanistan and to emphasize that the USA was not targeting Islam or even the population of Afghanistan, but rather Bin Laden and the members of his organization and the Taliban regime.

For military purposes the USA secured the cooperation of some of Afghanistan's neighbors, Pakistan, Uzbekistan and Tajikistan in order to deploy forces in their territory or at the very least operate from their airspace.

The majority of the American airforces and special forces were concentrated in the Indian Ocean in a task force of aircraft carriers and helicopters, and long range bombers were mobilized from the base in Diego Garcia.

The campaign in Afghanistan was structured in three principle stages:

- **First stage** – destruction of Taliban air defense and aircraft, immediately followed by a bombing campaign to destroy Taliban and Bin Laden government and military targets.
- **Second stage** – An extensive ground attack of the Northern Alliance forces with massive air support from the USA.
- **Third stage** – After destroying most of the Taliban's power and the conquest of most of the territory of Afghanistan by the Northern Alliance forces,

relatively extensive introduction of special forces in order to help the Northern Alliance destroy the Taliban and Al Qaida's last pockets of resistance and to search for Bin Laden and the Taliban leader Mullah Mohammed Omar.

The Taliban's collapse in the face of the American air strikes and the Northern Alliance's ground attack was surprisingly rapid and a large part of Afghanistan, including the capital Kabul, fell into the hands of the Northern Alliance after little or almost no military resistance.

Until now a limited number of points of resistance to the Northern Alliance onslaught have been evident in Mazar-e-Sharif, Kunduz, Kandahar and the hills of the Tora Bora region, where the fighting continues as these lines are being written.

It should be mentioned that the more determined fighting came from the Al Qaeda forces and "Arab Afghans" who fought alongside the Taliban, while Taliban forces usually hurried to surrender or reach agreement with the Northern Alliance forces.

As of this moment the war in Afghanistan has not yet ended. Fighting continues in a number of areas and Bin Laden and Mullah Mohammed Omar have not yet been captured, although the USA has already attained several significant achievements.

Firstly the Taliban regime, which gave its patronage to Bin Laden, has paid the full price and lost its political standing. This is an important message about what countries and regimes that support terror can anticipate.

Another important achievement was the destruction of the terror infrastructure established in Afghanistan by Bin Laden, eradication of a significant number of Islamic terrorists who were located in Afghanistan and the capture of many others which might facilitate interrogation and exposure of essential information in the continued struggle against Islamic terror.

Alongside the achievements however, there are still many unresolved problems:

The future of Afghanistan « during December extensive peace talks were held between different Afghan factions with regard to the establishment of a temporary government to assume rule of Afghanistan.

The talks ended successfully with the decision to establish a temporary government headed by Hamid Karazai (leader of the Pashtun tribe) that would incorporate some of the movements and different ethnic groups in Afghanistan. This government took office on December 22, 2001 and is expected to rule until general elections are held.

Already today there are various elements appealing their share in the temporary government and the disputes that have characterized Afghan society throughout modern history will apparently continue to pose a serious challenge to the establishment of a stable regime in this country in the future as well.

Bin Laden's international terror infrastructure « the battle in Afghanistan destroyed the infrastructure of Al Qaeda and other Islamic terror organizations in Afghanistan; however, these infrastructures are distributed throughout the Muslim world, as well as in the West and the USA. The battle against Islamic terror is therefore far from over.

The nature of the struggle as a cultural conflict « Bin Laden stressed that his struggle is a battle between Islamic culture and Judeo-Christian (Crusader) or Western culture.

In this context Bin Laden is the spearhead of radical Islam's struggle with its enemies, but most radical Islamic movements share this view and therefore the conflict is likely to go on even if Bin Laden is caught or killed in Afghanistan.

In conclusion, it appears that the battle in Afghanistan is only the first, albeit an important, chapter in the war against terror declared by the USA or the cultural conflict described by Huntington on the one hand and Bin Laden on the other.

Notes

Islamic Fundamentalism – Background

1. Bernard Lewis, "Islam and Liberal Democracy," *The Atlantic Monthly*, February 1993.
   Lawrence Kaplan (ed.), *Fundamentalism in Comparative Perspective*, University of Massachusetts Press, 1992, pp. 4-5.
2. Emanuel Sivan, *Islamic Fanatics*, Sifriat Ofakim, Tel Aviv, 1986, pp. 291-591; Lawrence Kaplan (ed.), *Fundamentalism in Comparative Perspective*, University of Massachusetts Press, 1992, pp. 6-7.
3. David Menashri, *Iran in Revolution*, Kibbutz Meuhad, Tel Aviv, 1998, pp. 203-205.
4. Martin Kramer, *Protest and Revolution in Shiite Islam*, Kibbutz Meuhad, Tel Aviv, 1985, pp. 11-15.
5. A.B. Lughud, *Arab Rediscovery of Europe*, Princeton Univ. Press, 1963 pp. 69-158. A. Hourani, *Arabic Thought in the Liberal Ages 1939-1978*, Oxford Univ. Press, 1962, pp. 34-102.
6. J. Waardenburg, "World Religions as Seen in the Light of Islam" in A. Walch and P. Cachia (eds.) *Islam Past Influence and Present Challenge*, Edinburgh Univ. Press, 1979, pp. 255-265.
7. Sayyid Qutb, *Mualem Fi el Tariq*, Damascus, pp. 124-126.
8. Chris Huri and Peter Chippendale, *What is Islam?*, Ahiassaf Publishers Ltd., Tel Aviv, 1991, pp. 92-93.
9. Hava Lazarus Yaffe, *More Conversations on the Islamic Religion*, Hebrew University of Jerusalem, Ministry of Defense Publications, pp. 92-97.
10. Chris Huri and Peter Chippendale, *What is Islam?*, Ahiassaf Publishers Ltd., Tel Aviv, 1991, pp. 93-94.

11. Emanuel Sivan, *Islamic Fanatics*, Sifriat Ofakim, Am Oved, Tel Aviv, 1986, pp. 94-95,103-114.
12. Ilan Pepe (Ed.), *Islam and Peace – Islamic Approaches to Peace in the Contemporary Arab World*, The Peace Research Institute, Givat Haviva, 1992, pp. 10-14.
13. Fuad Ajami, *The Arab Predicament*, Cambridge University Press, New York, pp. 63-77.
14. Hassan al Hadibi, *Dawa Wal Kawda*, Cairo, Dar Altaba a Wal Nashar el Ismaliya, 1977.
15. Al Mawdudi propounds his worldview in three main books: The Jihad in Islam, Islam and the Djahilia and Principles of Muslim Government.
16. Emanuel Sivan, *Islamic Fanatics*, Sifriat Ofakim, Am Oved, Tel Aviv, 1986, pp. 32-40.
17. *Aldawa*, July 1977, pp. 26-27.
18. Emanuel Sivan, *Islamic Fanatics*, Sifriat Ofakim, Am Oved, Tel Aviv, 1986, pp. 95-110.
19. For the characteristics of the period see: J. Wain, "Djahilia," *Encyclopedia of Islam*, Vol. 1, 1953, pp. 999-1000.
20. Sayyid Qutb, *Mualem Fi el Tariq*, Damascus, pp. 13-60.
21. Ibid., pp. 9, 224, 204.
22. Ibid., ???, p.120.
23. Ibid., ???, pp. 141-153, 171-175.
24. Sayyid Qutb, *El Adala*, Seventh Edition, pp. 25, 36, 81.
25. Sayyid Qutb, *Maalem Pi el Tarek*, Damascus, pp. 125-126.
26. Sayyid Qutb, *Djahilia*, p. 9.
27. Sayyid Qutb, *El Adala*, Seventh Edition, p. 258.
28. Emanuel Sivan, *Islamic Fanatics*, Sifriat Ofakim, Am Oved, Tel Aviv, 1986, pp. 95-110.
29. Sayyid Qutb is among those who laid the groundwork for research on the West by Islamic scholars.
30. G.E Von Gruneberg, *Islam: Essay on the Natural Growth of a Cultural Tradition*, London, 1969, p. 95.
31. Joseph Olmert, "The Shi'is and Lebanese State" in Martin Kramer, *Shi'is Resistance and Revolution*, Westview Press, Boulder, Colorado, 1987, pp. 189-198.
32. Emanuel. Sivan, *Radical Islam: Medieval Theory and Modern Politics*, New Haven Press, 1985.
33. Emanuel Sivan, *Islamic Fanatics*, Sifriat Ofakim, Am Oved, Tel Aviv, 1986, pp. 94-100.

34. Martin Kramer, *Protest and Revolution in Shiite Islam*, Kibbutz Meuhad, Tel Aviv, 1985, pp. 141-143.
    Hava Lazarus Yaffe, *More Conversations on the Islamic Religion*, Hebrew University of Jerusalem, Ministry of Defense Publications, pp. 92-97.
35. Hamid Algar, (trans), *Islam and Revolution Writings and Declarations of Iman Khomeini*, Berkeley, 1981.
36. Martin Kramer, *Protest and Revolution in Shiite Islam*, Kibbutz Meuhad, Tel Aviv, 1985, p.144.

Afghanistan – The Ethnic Structure

1. Rouhollah K. Ramzani, *The Northern Tier: Afghanistan, Iran and Turkey* D. Van Nostrand Company, Canada, 1996, pp. 28-32.
2. Wilber D.N. *Afghanistan*, New Haven, 1969, p. 56.
   Afghanistan, the CIA Fact Book.
3. Oliver Roy, "Ethnic Identity and Political Expressions in northern Afghanistan" in *Muslims in Central Asia, Expressions of Identity and Change*, Jo Ann Gross (ed.), Duke Univ. Press, Durham, and London 1992, pp. 74-75.
4. *Afghanistan*, The CIA fact book.
5. With regard to the definition of the term Qawm, see:
   Oliver Roy, *Islam and Resistance in Afghanistan*, Cambridge Univ. Press, 1986, chapter 1.
   Azoy Whitney, Buzkashi, *Game and Power in Afghanistan*, Univ. of Pennsylvania Press, 1982, pp. 31-32.
6. Oliver Roy, "Ethnic Identity and Political Expressions in Northern Afghanistan," in *Muslims in Central Asia: Expressions of Identity and Change*, Jo Ann Gross (ed.), Duke Univ. Press, Durham and London 1992, pp. 77-79.
7. *Afghanistan*, the CIA fact book.
8. Ibid.
9. *Afghanistan*, the CIA fact book.
10. Barbara F Grimes (ed.) *Ethnologue*, 13th edition, 1996.
11. Oliver Roy "Ethnic Identity," p. 73.
12. Barbara F Grimes (ed.) *Ethnologue*, 13th edition, 1996.
13. Dr. David Bannet (ed.) "The Hazara of Afghanistan," *Global Evangelization Movement*, N. Hamilton, 1996.
14. Ibid.
15. Ibid.

Historical Background – Milestones in the Formation of Afghanistan

1. In English, Dur-e-Duran means "pearl of pearls."
2. Haim Gerber, *Islam Guerilla War and Revolution*, Lynne Rienner, London, 1988, pp. 131-132.
3. Ibid., p. 132.
4. Mark Heller, *The Soviet Invasion of Afghanistan*, C.C.S. Memorandum No. 2, March 82, pp. 1-2.

The Role of Mohammed Daoud

1. Haim Gerber, *Islam Guerilla War and Revolution*, Lynne Rienner, London 1988, p. 134.
2. Hanna Negaran, "Afghanistan: A Marxist Regime in Muslim Society," *Current History*, Vol. 76 No. 446, April 1979.
3. Louis Dupree "Afghanistan under the Khalq," *Problems of Communism*, Vol. XXVIII 4 (July – August 1979), pp. 34-50.
4. Mark Heller, *The Soviet Invasion of Afghanistan* C.C.S Memorandum No. 2, March 1982, pp. 1-2.
5. Ibid., p. 135.
6. Taraki was cultural attachù to the U.S.A. and in the 1960s even served as translator for the U.S. Embassy in Kabul. In the late 1950s Hafezullah Amin studied at Columbia University in the USA.
7. H. Beattle "Effect of soar revolution in the Nahrin area of Northern Afghanistan" in Shahrani and Confield, *Revolution and Rebellion*s, pp.184-208.
8. The Friendship Agreement between the USSR and Afghanistan signed on December 5, 1978.
9. Mark Heller, *The Soviet Invasion of Afghanistan*, C.S.S Memorandum No. 2, March 82, p. 7.
10. Brezhnev's declaration in the media following the invasion of Afghanistan.
11. Richardson .J.C, *Conclusions on Management of the Afghan Crisis*.
12. Antony Arnold, *Afghanistan's Two Party Communism: Parcham and Khalq*, Stanford Hoover Institute Press, 1983, chapters 1-7.
13. Anthony Arnold, "Soviet Relations with Afghanistan" in *Domestic Determinants of Soviet Foreign Policy towards South Asia and the Middle East*, Hafez Malik (ed.) St. Martin's Press, N.Y., 1990, pp. 200-201.

The Soviet Invasion and the Karmal Government

1. Anthony Arnold, "Soviet Relations with Afghanistan" in *Domestic Determinants of Soviet Foreign Policy towards South Asia and the Middle East*, Hafez Malik (ed.) St. Martin's Press, N.Y., 1990, pp. 200-201.
2. *Washington Post*, April 17, 1988, p. 30.
3. *Kabul New Times*, December 22, 1985.
4. Richard F. Staar (ed.) 1987, *Yearbook on International Communist Affairs*, Stanford Hoover Institute Press, 1987, p. 417.

The Government of Najib (Najibullah)

1. Vladimir Moskalenko, "Relations with India / Pakistan and Afghan problem" in *Domestic Determinants of Soviet Foreign Policy towards South Asia and the Middle East*, Hafez Malik (ed.) St. Martin's Press, N.Y., 1990, p. 137.
2. *Kabul New Times*, May 13, 1988.
3. *Kabul New Times*, May 13-14, 1988.
4. Richard F. Staar (ed.) 1987 *Year book on International Communist Affairs*, Stanford Hoover Institution press, 1987, p. 397.
5. Ibid.
6. *Kabul New Times*, June 15, 1987.

The Fall of Najibullah's Regime and the Rise of the Mujahidin

1. Anthony Arnold, "Soviet Relations with Afghanistan," in *Domestic Determinants of Soviet Foreign Policy towards South Asia and the Middle East*, Hafez Malik (ed.) St. Martin's Press, N.Y., 1990, pp. 200-204.
2. *The Middle East*, June 1992.
3. *Negavisimia Gazeta*, May 8, 1993.
4. *Jane's Defense Weekly*, September 8, 1994.
5. *The Middle East*, June 1992.

Afghanistan – Islamic Opposition and the Mujahidin Movements

1. Huntington Samuel, *The Clash of Civilizations and the Remaking of World Order*, Simon and Schuster, N.Y., 1996.
2. *The Middle East*, September 1992.

3. Anderei Prnov, *Izvestiia*, July 3, 1992.
4. Robert Canfield "Afghanistan: The Trajectory of Internal Alignments" *Middle East Journal*, vol. 43, no. 2 (Autumn 89) pp. 642-643.
5. Edgar O'Balance, *Afghanistan Wars 1834-1992*, 1933 Brasseys, London, 1993.
6. J. Bruce Amstutz, *Afghanistan The First Five Years of Soviet Occupation*, National Defense University, Washington, D.C., 1986, pp. 116-118.
7. *The Middle East*, September 1992.
8. On Pakistani involvement in the civil war in Afghanistan see:
   Shiel Tefft, *Christian Science Monitor*, June 20, 1990.
   Marvin G. Wienbaum, "War and Peace in Afghanistan: the Pakistani role" *Middle East Journal*, Vol. 45, No. 1, Winter '91.
9. Marvin G. Wienbaum, "War and Peace in Afghanistan: The Pakistani role." *Middle East Journal*, Vol. 45, No. 1, Winter '92.
10. J. Bruce Amstutz, *Afghanistan The First Five Years of Soviet Occupation*, National Defense University, Washington, D.C., 1986, pp. 97-101.
11. Jo Ann Gross (ed.) *Muslims in Central Asia – Expressions of Identity and Change*, Duke University Press, 1991, p. 81.

Leaders of the Mujahidin Movements in Afghanistan

1. Chantal Lobato; "Kabul 1987-1988: Communist and Islam" in *Religions in Communist Lands*, Keston College Press, 1991.
2. Jo Ann Gross (ed.) *Muslims in Central Asia – Expressions of Identity and Change*, Duke University Press, 1991, p. 81.
3. Ibid., pp. 99-100.
4. *FBIS – Middle East and North Africa Daily Report*, February 6, 1980.
5. Van Dyk, *In Afghanistan: An American Odyssey*, New York, Coward McCann Inc., 1983, p. 63.
6. *FBIS – Middle East and North Africa Daily Report*, February 6, 1980.
7. Van Dyk, *In Afghanistan: An American Odyssey*, New York, Coward McCann Inc., 1983, p. 63.
8. *Washington Post*, October 22, 1983.

Military Leadership of the Mujahidin

1. FBIS – Middle East North Africa Daily Report, October 22, 1983.
2. Ibid.

3. JPRS – NEAR East/North Africa Report, September 11, 1980, p. 7.
4. J. Bruce Amstutz, Afghanistan The First Five Years of Soviet Occupation, National Defense University, Washington, D.C., 1986, pp. 97-98.
5. Edgar O'Balance, Afghan Wars 1839-1992, What Britain Gave up and the Soviet Union Lost, Brasseys, London, 1993, pp. 216-217.

The Mujahidin Regime of Rabbani

1. M. Hassan Kakar, Afghanistan, University of California Press, Berkeley, 1995, pp. 288-289.
2. Jane's Defense Weekly, May 8, 1993.
3. M. Hassan Kakar, Afghanistan, University of California Press, Berkeley, 1995, pp. 289-290.

The Taliban Movement – Roots and Ideology
The Taliban and the Road to Power

1. The school in Deobund was established in 1867 by Mohammed Abid Hussein and was the leading Islamic religious school in India. The school's ideology was influenced in the 18th century by the doctrine of Shah Walli Allah and at the beginning of the 19th century by the Wahabiya movement in India. The Deobundis adopted, in the spirit of these beliefs, a strict, puritanical Islamic orthodox approach and launched a fierce struggle against all streams and interpretations that refused to accept their approach.
2. The Hanfiya, one of four school of interpretation of Islamic law. The Hanfiya is based on the position of the Imam Abu Hanifa (700-767) and has become the accepted interpretation today in central Asia, India, Pakistan, Turkey, and in some of the states that were under Ottoman rule.
3. *The Straits Times*, December 10, 1996.
4. Jamiya-el-ulama-islamiya (J.U.I).
   Time Magazine, November 4, 1996, vol. 148, No. 21.
5. Ahmed Rashid, Taliban, Militant Islam, Oil and Fundamentalism in Central Asia, Yale University Press, New Haven, 2000, pp. 26-27.
6. Franz Schurmann, "Afghanistan's Taliban Rebels Blend Islam and Maoism" *Pacific News Service - Jinn Magazine*, September 96.
7. An article by Professor Musa Maarufi, past deputy dean of the faculty of law

and political science at the University of Kabul. American Educational Trust, 1999.
8. *Pakistan Today*, October 3, 1997.

The Taliban and the Road to Power

1. *Dow Jones News*, September 21, 1997.
2. *Pakistan Today*, October 3, 1997.
3. *The Straits Times*, October 15 1996.
4. *The Straits Times*, October 13 1996.
5. AFP – September 22, 1997.
6. AP – May, 25, 1997.
7. *Dawn*, July 14, 1997.
8. *Asia Week*, May 30, 1997.
9. CNN – August 25, 1999.
10. *Washington Post*, October 1, 1997.
    Dawn, July 14, 1997.

The Taliban Regime – Main Characteristics

1. *The Washington Post*, October 1, 1997.
2. AP, September 27, 1997. CNN, September 27, 1997.
3. On the situation of women in Afghanistan see the Amnesty reports: *Women in Afghanistan: Pawns in Men's Power Struggles*, ASA 11/11/99, November 1999; *Women in Afghanistan: The Violations Continue*, ASA 11/05/97, June 1997.
4. *Irish Times*, October 1, 1997.
5. *Pakistan Today*, November 7, 1997.
6. "Facts and Reality under Taliban Rule – Information from," Taliban government version as it appears on the government website, Afghanistan Today.
7. With regard to the infraction of minority rights see the Amnesty report: *Afghanistan: The Human Rights of Minorities*, ASA 11/14/99, November 1999.
8. The Foreign Minister of the Taliban government claimed that his country was opposed to the cultivation and trade of opium and drugs because the religion forbids it, and that his government therefore works to reduce the

phenomenon of opium cultivation and smuggling it across the country's borders. *Kabul Times*, June 19, 2000.
9. Economist, October 20, 2001, quoted in Maariv.

The Anti-Taliban Coalition – The Northern Alliance

1. *The Straits Times*, October 12, 1996.
2. An article on the internet by Musa Maarufi, past deputy dean of the faculty of law and political science at the University of Kabul.
America, Education Trust, April, 1998.
3. *New York Times*, October 5, 1997.
4. The Taliban government's Internet site. It is not clear whether there is any truth in this information or whether it is Taliban propaganda meant to cause a rift in the ranks of the opposition.
5. AFP, September 22, 1997.
6. Reuters reported from Kabul that the Taliban closed the Iranian embassy and deported the diplomats on charges of espionage.
Afghanistan Islamic Press (AIP), June 3, 1997.
Reuters, June 3, 1997.
7. *Pakistan Today*, October 24, 1997.
8. AP, August 10, 1998.
9. Tabloid News Services, August 13, 1998.

Internal Power Struggles Among the Uzbekis

1. *Asia Week*, May 30,1997.
2. AP, May 20, 1997.
3. *Asia Week*, May 30, 1997.
4. AP, May 25, 1997.
5. *Pakistan Today*, November 21, 1997.
6. *Pakistan Today*, November 21, 1997.
7. *Pakistan Today*, October 24, 1997.
8. AP, November 24, 1997.

Involvement of Outside Agents in the Civil War in Afghanistan

1. Ahmed Rashid, Taliban, Militant Islam, Oil and Fundamentalism in Central Asia, Yale University Press, New Haven 2000, pp 157-159.
2. At a press conference on June 19, 2000, the Taliban Foreign Minister claimed that his country is not involved in the training and support of Mujahidin active in the C.I.S. in general or in Chechniya and Uzbekistan in particular. *Kabul Times*, June 19, 2000, *Afghanistan Today*, August 1, 2000. Taliban leader Mullah Omar warned the USSR against taking action against his country and denied any connection or involvement with the Mujahidin in Chechniya. *Kabul Times*, June 21, 2000.
3. In an interview, the head of the Ministry of Information and Culture, Mullah Abed El Hai Matmayan, warned Russia of military action against Afghanistan, saying that "the fate of Russia will be similar to the fate of the USSR that came before it." He also claimed Afghanistan's right to recognize the Chechniyan state and that Russia itself had done so in 1996. BBC interview in June 2000.
4. The Taliban Foreign Minister warned Russia lest she employ force against Afghanistan and recommended that it remember the lesson of its past involvement, saying that Afghanistan was ready to teach Russia another lesson if it took action against it. *Kabul Times*, June 19, 2000.
5. Ahmed Rashid, Taliban, Militant Islam Oil and Fundamentalism in Central Asia, Yale University Press, New Haven 2000, pp 143-156.
6. The Taliban leader, Mullah Mohammed Omar, accused the USA of seeking control over the natural resources in the region and therefore wielding its influence on Tajikistan and Uzbekistan. According to him, Russia is working to reduce this American influence by strengthening its ties with these governments by means of false allegations of Afghan threat to their welfare and the need for Russian military aid in order to avert the danger. *Kabul Times*, June 21, 2000.
7. A.P, March 21, 1999.

Pakistan – Afghanistan (Taliban) Relations

1. Masud forces in the Panjir valley presented to western journalists Pakistani captives who had been taken in battles with the Taliban. These prisoners testified to their recruitment by Pakistani intelligence to fight on the Taliban side.
The Magazine, November 4,1996, vol.148, No. 21.

2. In September 1996 the Pakistani Minister of Internal Affairs, Nasrallah Babar, visited Kabul shortly after it was conquered by the Taliban to coordinate subsequent moves and relations.
3. *Pakistan Today*, November 14, 1997.
4. *Dow Jones News*, November 18, 1997.
5. Ahmed Rashid, *Foreign Affairs*, Nov.-Dec., 1999.

Diplomatic Moves to Resolve the Conflict in Afghanistan

1. CNN news – U.N envoy meets with Afghanistan's Taliban, September 29, 1996.
2. *New York Times*, September 28, 1997.
3. Ahmed Rashid, Taliban, Militant Islam, Oil and Fundamentalism in Central Asia, Yale University Press, New Haven 2000, p 204.
4. Ibid.
5. AP, March 5, 1999.
6. Ahmed Rashid, *Foreign Affairs*, Nov.-Dec., 1999.

"Afghan Terror" in the International Arena as a Reflection of Cultural Conflict

1. Samuel Huntington, "The Clash of Civilizations?" *Foreign Affairs*, Summer 1993.
2. Samuel Huntington, *The Clash of Civilizations and the Remaking of the World Order*, Simon and Schuster, N.Y., 1996.
3. Samuel Huntington, "The Clash of Civilizations?" *Foreign Affairs*, Summer 1993.
4. Ibid.
5. Huntington cites William Lind, ibid., p. 9.
6. Ibid., p. 23
7. Huntington also refers to the USSR as part of western culture and ideology.
8. At the time of writing, there was tension between the Serbs and Albanian Muslims in Kosovo.

International Terror – Theoretical Background

1. Martha Crenshow, *Terrorism, Legitimacy and Power*, Wesleyan University, Middletown, 1983.
2. Ibid., p.3.
3. Ibid., p.1.
4. Ibid., p.2.
5. Alex Schmidt, *Political Terrorism*, Transaction Books, New Brunswick, 1983.
6. Ibid., p.110.
7. Ibid., p.111.
8. Rand Corporation, *Chronology of International Terrorism*.
9. Interate Project, *International Terrorism: Attributes of Terrorism Events*.
10. Boaz Ganor, *Defining Terrorism*, The Interdisciplinary Center, Herzliya, vol. 4, August 1998, pp. 22-21.
11. Paul Wilkinson, *Terrorism and the Liberal State*, Macmillan Education Ltd., 1977, p. 182.
12. Ray S. Cline and Yona Alexander, *Terrorism as State-Sponsored Covert Warfare*, Fairfax, Virginia, 1986.
13. Walter Laquer, *Terrorism*, Little Brown, Boston, 1997.
14. Shaul Kunstler, *International Terror, Ideology, Organization, and Operation*, Am Oved, Tel Aviv University.

"Cultural Terror"

1. Rand Corporation, Chronology of International Terrorism.
2. Interate Project, International Terrorism: Attributes of Terrorism Events.

The Destruction of the Statues of Buddha at Bamian

1. *Yediot Aharonot*, March 4, 2001.
2. *Maariv*, March 4, 2001.
3. BBC News Online, October 20, 2000.
4. *Maariv*, March 12, 2001.
5. *Maariv*, March 4, 2001.
6. AP News Agency, March 17, 2001.
7. AP News Agency, March 16, 2001.
   AP News Agency, March 19, 2001.
8. Reuters News Agency, March 23, 2001.

Afghan Terror in the International Arena

1. According to an article in the weekly *Al-Usbu al-Arabi* the number of people was 12,000. *Al Usbu al-Arabi*, July 1992.
2. *Intelligence Newsletter* (France) – July 9, 1992.
   Jean Goodwin, *Firetrap*, Gestalt Haifa Ltd., 1989.
3. *Conflict International*, April 1994.
4. Haim Raviv, *Bamahaneh*, August 1992.
5. *Al Wasat*, London, February 15, 1993.
6. *Al Wasat*, London, February 15, 1993.
7. Yoram Schweitzer, "Middle East Terrorism: The Afghan Alumni, Military Balance in the Middle East 1999-2000," Jaffee Center for Strategic Studies, MIT Press 2000.
8. *Al Sabah* (Tunisia), January 22, 1992.
9. *Conflict International*, April 1994.
10. *Al Aharam* (Egypt), August 30, 1992.
11. French News Agency (AFP), February 11, 1992.
12. *Le Matin* (Algeria) December 4, 1991, French News Agency (AFP) from Algeria December 8, 1991.
13. *Conflict International*, April, 1994
14. *Conflict International*, July/August, 1994
15. *Conflict International*, April, 1998
16. AFP, October 17, 1999.
17. AFP, August 9, 1999.
18. *Al-Hayat*, May 5, 1999.
19. *Intelligence Newsletter* (France) – July 9, 1992.
20. *Al Wasat*, London, June 5, 1993.
21. *Ahir Sa'ah*, Cairo, August 22, 1993.
22. *Al Aharam*, Cairo, June 10, 1993.
23. *Ruz al Yusif*, Cairo, July 19, 1993.
24. *Al Aharam*, Egypt, December 4, 1993.
25. *Jane's Intelligence Review Yearbook 1993*
26. *Al Sharq*, (Qatar), July 27, 1992.
27. *Al Gumhuriyya*, Cairo, August 20, 1993.

Naziah Nitzhi Rashid, one of the assassins of the Egyptian Minister of Internal Affairs, carried a fake identity document that was produced in Afghanistan.
28. *Al Arabi*, Egypt, November 27, 1993.
29. *Al Wafd*, Egypt, November 20, 1993.
30. *Alaharam*, Egypt, November 21, 1993.
31. *Jane's Intelligence Review Yearbook 1993*
32. *Shihan*, Jordan, March 19, 1994.
33. Tal Nahman, *Conflict at Home, Egypt and Jordan Facing Extremist Islam*, Papyrus, Tel Aviv University, 1999, p. 208.
34. *New York Times* Internet Edition, January 29, 2000.
35. AFP, February 29, 1999.
36. AFP, quoting ABC network from January 21, 2000.
37. Tal Nahman, Conflict at home, Egypt and Jordan Facing Extremist Islam, Papyrus, Tel Aviv University 1999, p 208.
38.
39. AFP, quoting ABC network from February 29, 2000.
40. *Kol Ha'Ir*, March 25, 2000.
41. *Haaretz*, August 22, 2000.
42. Conflict International, April 1994.
43. Internet. http://www/azzam/com. November 20, 1999.
44. *Ahir Sa'ah* (Cairo), June, 10, 1993.
45. Ahmed Rashid, Taliban, Militant Islam, Oil and Fundamentalism in Central Asia, Yale University Press, New Haven 2000, p 131.
46. Ibid, p 134.
47. "Interpreting the Broader Context and Meaning of Bin-Laden's Fatwa" Magnus Ranstorp, *Studies in Conflict Terrorism*, vol. 21, October-December 1998.
48. Eli Karmon, "Terrorism a' la Bim Laden is not a Peace Process Problem", Policy Watch, Washington Institute for Near East Policy, No 347, October 28, 1998.
49. "Bin-Laden and the Problem of State-Supported Terrorism," David K. Schenker, *Policy Watch*, Washington Institute for Near East Policy, No.346, October 21, 1998.
50. Ibid.
51. "American Soldiers Are Paper Tigers – Interview," *Middle East Quarterly*, Vol.V, No. 4, December 1998.
52. *Al Hayat*, August 6, 1998.
53. *Al Hayat*, February 12, 1999.

54. Yossef Bodansky, *Bin Laden, The Man who Declared War on America*, Forum, Roseville, California, 1999, pp. 346-347.
55. Ibid, pp. 328-331.
56. *Haaretz*, August 27, 2000.
    Maariv, August 27, 2000.
    Yediot Aharonot, August 27, 2000.

Appendix

Appendix A

Afghanistan – Provincial Divisions

Afghanistan is divided into 30 provinces and another seven administrative regions.

- ☐ Badakhshan – (Feyzabad)
- ☐ Badghis – (Qaleh-ye Now)
- ☐ Baghlan – (Baglan)
- ☐ Balkh – (Mazar-e-Shariff)
- ☐ Bamian – (Bamian)
- ☐ Farah – (Farah)
- ☐ Faryab – (Meymaneh)
- ☐ Ghazni – (Ghazni)
- ☐ Ghowr – (Chaghcharan)
- ☐ Helmand – (Lashkar Gah)
- ☐ Herat – (Herat)
- ☐ Jowzjan – (Sheberghan)
- ☐ Kabul – (Kabul)
- ☐ Kandahar – (Kandahar)
- ☐ Kapisa – (Mahmud-e-Raqi)
- ☐ Konar – (Asadabad)
- ☐ Kunduz – (Qonduz)
- ☐ Laghman – (Mehtar Lam)
- ☐ Lowgar – (Baraki Barak)
- ☐ Nangarhar – (Jalalabad)
- ☐ Nimruz – (Zaranj)
- ☐ Oruzgan – (Tarin Kowt)
- ☐ Paktia – (Gardez)
- ☐ Paktika – (Zareh Sharan)
- ☐ Parwan – (Charikar)
- ☐ Samangan – (Aybak)
- ☐ Sar-i Pol
- ☐ Takhar – (Taloqan)
- ☐ Wardak – (Kowt-e-Ashrow)
- ☐ Zabol – (Qalat)
- ☐ Nuristan (possible addition)
- ☐ Khost (possible addition)

The central cities in Afghanistan are:
- Kabul – the capital;
- Kandahar – the largest city in the south of the country and the spiritual and administrative center of the Taliban movement;
- Herat – the largest city in the west of the country;
- Mazar-e-Sharif – the largest city in the northwest of the country;
- Jalalabad – the largest city in the east of the country.

Appendix B

1979 As A Watershed in the History of Afghanistan

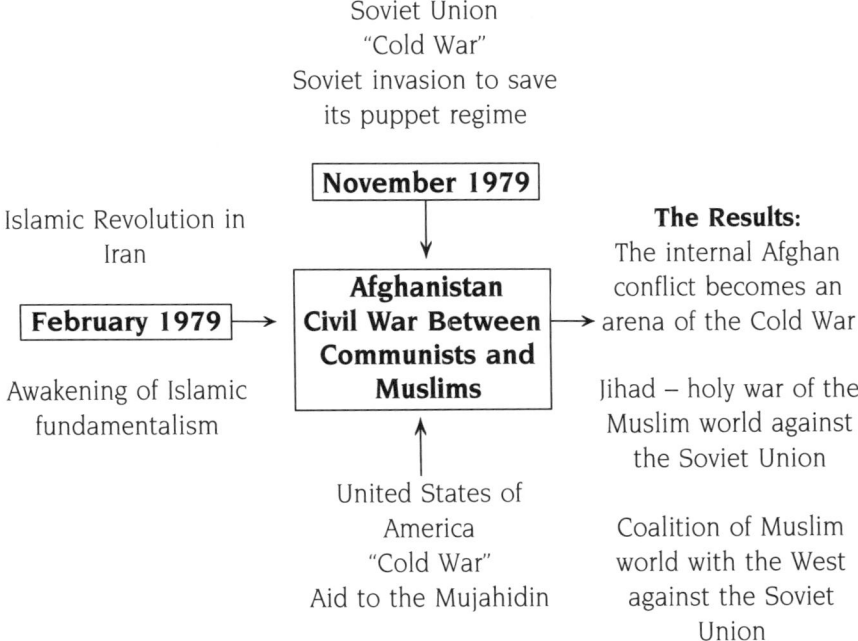

Appendix C

The Taliban Regime – Central Position Holders

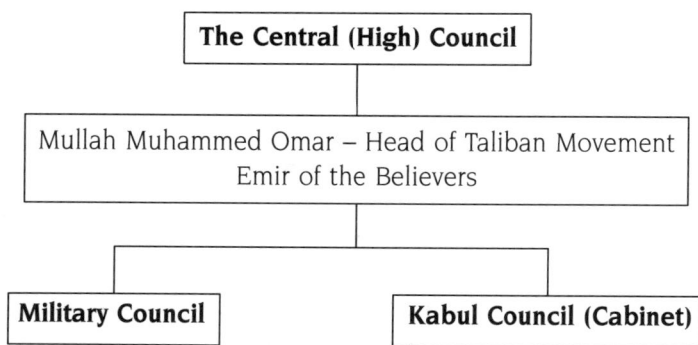

Composition of the High Council (as of 1997)

Taliban leader Emir of Believers	Mullah Mohammed Omar
Chairman of Governing Council Deputy leader of Taliban	Mullah Mohammed Rabbani
	Mullah Mohammed Ghaus
	Mullah Abdul Jalil
Chief of Staff	Mullah Mohammed Hassan
Chief of Army Corps	Mullah Mohammed Fazil
Minister of Information	Mullah Ghiasuddin Agha
Minister of the Interior	Mullah Khairullah Khairkhwa
Head of Legal System	Mullawi Abed El Sattar Sanani
Head of Central Bank	Mullah Ahsanullah Ehsan

Composition of Military Council (as of 1997)

High commander	Mullah Mohammed Omar
Chief of staff	Mullah Mohammed Hassan
Chief of army	Mullah Rahmat Allah
Commander of army corps	Mullah Mohammed Fazil
Division commander	Mullah Jumaa Khan
Division commander	Mullah Mohammed Younas

Composition of Military Council (as of 1997) – Continue

Division commander	Mullah Mohammed Gul
Division commander	Mullah Mohammed Aziz Khan
Commander of armored force No.4	Mullah Mohammed Zahir

Composition of the Kabul Council (as of 1997)

Foreign Minister	Mullah Wakil Ahmed Moutowakil
Health Minister	Mullah Mohammed Abbas
Minister of the Interior	Mullah Abdur Razzaq
Minister of Construction	Mullah Ubeidullah
Finance Minister	Mullah Taher Anwari
Minister of Culture and Information	Mullah Qodratullah
Minister of Agriculture	Mullah Abed El Latif Mansur
Minister of Energy and Water	Mullah Mohammed Essa
Minister of Communication	Mulana Ahmadullah Muti
Minister of Justice	Mullah Nurrudin Turabi
Minister of Higher Education	Mullaui Hamdullah Numani
Minister of Home Affairs	Mullaui Jalal El Din Hakani
Minister of Planning	Quari Din Mohammed

Key Figures in Various Governmental Authorities

Government leaders and provincial governors	
Head of Kabul Council	Mullah Mohammed Rabbani
Responsible for provincial administration	Mullah Ahsanullah
Governor of Kandahar province	Mullah Mohammed Hassan
Governor of Fakita province	Mullah Karmantullah
Fakita governor	Mullah Shamsaddin
Political leader in Lagur	Mullah Mohammed Ghaus
Foreign Ministry and Embassies	
Foreign Minister (current)	Mullah Wakil Ahmed Mutowakil
Afghan ambassador to Pakistan	Mullah Abed El Salam Zaif
Deputy Afghan ambassador to Pakistan	Suahil Shahdin

Key Figures in Various Governmental Authorities – Continue

Other ministers and position holders	
Minister for Refugee Rehabilitation	Mullah Abed el Raqib
Minister for handling matters involving deaths and injuries	Mullah Abed el Bak
Head of security services	Mullah Fadel Ahmed
Taliban spokesmen:	Mullawi Hakani
	Mullah Mohammed Abas

Appendix D

The Islamic Ring of Conflict

Muslim Countries with Secular Governments confronted by Fundamentalist Islamic Subversion

Egypt – Muslim Brotherhood, Islamic Jihad, Jamaat-e-Islami, etc.
Jordan – Muslim Brotherhood.
Syria – Muslim Brotherhood.
Lebanon – Hizbullah (Shiite), radical Sunni organizations, etc.
Iraq – El Dawa (Shiite) and other radical Sunni and Shiite organizations.
Saudi Arabia – Hizbullah (Shiite) and other radical Sunni and Shiite organizations.
Kuwait – radical Shiite organizations.
Bahrain – radical Shiite organizations.
Yemen – Islamic Jihad and other radical organizations.
Libya – Muslim Brotherhood and radical Sunni organizations.
Tunisia – Al Nahada.
Algeria – Extremist Islamic organizations such as the GIA and others – are engaged in a civil war.
Morocco – radical Sunni organizations.
Turkey – extremist Islamic organizations, extremist Shiite and Sunni organizations.
Tajikistan – extremist Sunni organizations.
Uzbekistan – extremist Sunni organizations.
China – separatist Islamic organizations of the Ivgorian minority.
Pakistan – radical Islamic opposition organizations.
Bangladesh – radical Islamic opposition organizations.
Malaysia – radical Islamic organizations.
Indonesia – radical Islamic organizations.
The Palestinian Authority – Hamas and Islamic Jihad.
The Muslim Autonomy in the Philippines – The MILF organization – extremist Islamic organization.

Muslim Minorities are struggling for Autonomy / Independence in the following places:

Bosnia (ex-Yugoslavia), Kosovo (ex-Yugoslavia), Chechniya (ex-USSR), Daghastan (ex-USSR), the Kashmir region in India, and the Zinjiang region in western China.

Struggles against Ethnic/Cultural Minorities Demanding Autonomy or Independence in Muslim Countries

Sudan – wars between the Muslim government and the Christian minority in the south of the country.

Indonesia – war between the central Muslim government and the Christian inhabitants of East Timor who are demanding independence, and oppression of the Chinese minority.

Conflicts and Wars Between Muslim Countries and Other Countries Along the Lines of Contact Between Islam and Other Cultures

The Israeli-Arab conflict.
Conflicts between Sudan and Uganda, Ethiopia (Christian).
War between Eritrea and Ethiopia (Christian).
Conflict between Turkey and Greece (Christian).
Conflict between Iraq and the USA and the West.
Conflict between Azerbaijan and Armenia (Christian).
The conflict between Afghanistan and Russia and its allies Tajikistan and Uzbekistan.
War between Pakistan and India (Kashmir region).

Appendix E

Prominent Acts of Terror Attributed to the "Afghan Alumni"

Sept. 1992 – Two terrorist attacks on a hotel in Aden occupied by western tourists.

Feb. 1993 – Explosion of car bomb in the Twin Towers in New York.

Dec. 1993 – Explosion on an Air France flight in Algeria by the G.I.A.

June 1995 – Attempted assassination of President Mubarak of Egypt in Ethiopia by the Jamaat-e-Islami

July-Oct. 1995 – Wave of terror in France by the GIA.

Oct. 1995 – Explosion of car bomb by the Jamaat-e-Islami in Riaka, Croatia.

Nov. 1995 – Assassination of an Egyptian diplomat in Switzerland by the "Egyptian Islamic Jihad."

Nov. 1995 – Explosion at the Egyptian embassy in Pakistan by suicide bombers from the Jamiya el Islamiya.

Nov. 1997 – Murder of fifty-eight western tourists at Luxor by Jamiya el Islamiya.

Aug. 1998 – Two car bombs at the USA embassies in Tanzania and Kenya by Al Qaida.

Oct. 2000 – Explosion of a boat-bomb alongside the U.S. destroyer "Cole" at the port of Aden in Yemen.

Sept. 2001 – Two hijacked airplanes successively crash into the twin towers in New York and cause their collapse. A third hijacked airplane crashes simultaneously into the Pentagon in Washington and a fourth crashes in Pennsylvania, apparently on its way to strike the presidential compound at Camp David.

Index of Names and Concepts

A
Abu Hamza 128
Abu Zbayda 135
Ahmed Khan 27
Ahmed Shah 21
Al Mihdar 128
Al Nahada 171
Al Qaeda 124, 131, 134, 139-144, 146, 148-149
Albania 107, 109, 131, 133, 142-143, 160
Algeria 124-128, 132-134, 137, 162, 171, 173
Ashura 18
Azerbaijan 107, 136, 143, 172

B
Bagram 37, 79, 83
Balkan 146
Bamian 116-121, 161, 165
Bosnia 107, 109, 124, 127, 137, 139-140, 171
Britain 22, 27-28, 126, 135, 142-143, 156

Buddha 116-121, 161

C
Chechnya 107, 124-125, 136-137, 140
China 8, 19, 40, 107-108, 117, 171

D
Dawa 137, 151, 171
Djahilia 15-17, 151
Durani 27, 29

E
Egypt 13-15, 17, 28, 59, 124, 128-133, 141-144, 162-163, 171, 173
El Abdin 135
Ethiopia 107, 131, 172-173

F
Faryab 91-93, 165
France 118, 126-127, 133-134, 162, 173

G
Gardez 165

[174]

Germany 118, 126, 143-144
Ghanzi 81

H
Herat 23, 45, 66, 74, 78, 80, 82, 103, 165-166
Hizb-e-Islam 54, 58-61, 66, 68-69, 90, 97, 123
Hizbullah 17, 55-56, 134, 171

I
Ibn Al Qutb 137
Ibn Timea 13, 15
India 13-14, 28-29, 96, 99, 107-108, 118-120, 144, 147, 154, 156, 171-172
Indonesia 107, 171-172
Iran 8-9, 17, 19, 21-22, 25, 27-28, 32, 36-37, 40, 45, 49, 55-57, 60, 68, 70, 79-80, 84, 86, 88-90, 92-95, 99-101, 104, 108-109, 113, 118, 123-125, 136, 150, 152, 158, 167
Iraq 49, 107, 132, 134, 141, 143-144, 171-172
Islamabad 45, 97, 99, 103-104
Ismael Khan 66, 82
Israel 107, 126, 133-135, 141, 172

J
Jalalabad 67, 79, 83, 103, 139, 165-166
Jamiya el Islamiya 173
Jordan 124, 132-135, 163, 171

K
Kabul 7, 9, 21, 23, 25-26, 29, 33, 36-46, 48-53, 55-56, 58-62, 64-66, 68-70, 72-74, 77-79, 81-87, 89, 91-92, 97-98, 101, 103, 117-118, 123, 128, 139, 148, 153-160, 165-166, 168-169
Kandahar 27, 72-73, 76, 78, 80-81, 103, 139, 148, 165-166, 169
Kashmir 96, 107, 124, 140, 146, 171-172
Kenya 96, 140, 142-143, 173
Khalq 22, 32-35, 41-43, 50, 153
Khomeini 8, 17-18, 37, 40, 49, 55-56, 60, 100-101, 109, 152
Kosovo 107, 109, 124, 137, 139-140, 160, 171

L
Libya 60, 171
London 128, 143, 151-153, 155-156, 162
Luxor 130, 132, 173

M
Macedonia 137
Mainama 92
Mashad 89
Mazar-e-Sharif 29, 74, 79-80, 83, 89, 92, 148, 165-166

N
Nadir Shah 27
Najaf 17
Najib (Najibullah) 42, 154
National Liberation Front 46, 55, 63
Northern Alliance 87, 103, 147-148, 158

P
Pakistan 8-9, 19, 21-22, 24, 28, 32, 40, 43-44, 49, 53-60, 64-65, 70-72, 75, 78-79, 82, 86, 94-99, 102, 104, 107, 118, 123, 125, 129, 131,

133-135, 138, 140-142, 147, 154-160, 169, 171-173
Palestinians 132, 134-136, 141
Panjshir 79, 89
Parcham 22, 32-36, 42, 50, 153
Pashtuns 19, 21-23, 67, 76
Peshawar 46, 57-62, 72, 98-99, 123-124, 129
Philippines 107-108, 140, 171
Prague 37-38

R
Rishkor 82
Russia 9, 27-28, 59, 79, 88, 90, 92, 95-96, 98, 101, 104-105, 107, 136-137, 159, 172

S
Saduzai 27
Serbia 108, 137
Somalia 139-141
Soviet Union 7, 19, 107, 109, 138, 156, 167
Sudan 107-108, 123-124, 129, 137-140, 142-143, 172

T
Takfir 17, 125
Talia 15-16
Tanzania 96, 140, 142, 173
The Hazaras 19, 25
The Islamic Party 54, 90
The UN 44, 102-103
Tunisia 102, 124-125, 127, 162, 171
Turkey 28, 79-80, 92, 107, 152, 156, 171-172

U
UN 35, 43-46, 84, 99, 102-104, 133, 137, 140, 145
USA 7-9, 32, 37, 40, 43-44, 50, 56-57, 60-62, 86, 89, 95-96, 104, 109, 147-149, 153, 159, 172-173

W
Wahab 13, 136, 156

Y
Yemen 123-124, 127-128, 138, 140, 171, 173

Z
Zain 135

DATE DUE

Demco, Inc. 38-293